New!
Revised
Edition

Latin *for* Children

— PRIMER A —

Classical or Ecclesiastical
Pronunciation

Dr. Aaron Larsen
Dr. Christopher Perrin

Latin for Children Primer A • *ANSWER KEY*

© Classical Academic Press®, 2017
Version 4.0
New, Revised Edition June 2017

ISBN: 978-1-60051-001-4

Classical Academic Press
515 S. 32nd Street
Camp Hill, PA 17011

www.ClassicalAcademicPress.com

Book and cover design: David Gustafson
Illustrations: Melissa Manwill

How to Teach
Latin for Children Primer A

A Suggested Schedule

This is a basic weekly schedule, taking approximately thirty minutes per day, to be modified as necessary by the teacher.

1

Day One: Present the paradigm (grammar chant) and vocabulary, and introduce the grammar from the Grammar Lesson. The students should chant through the paradigm and vocabulary two to three times. Watch the video.

2

Day Two: Review the paradigm (grammar chant) and vocabulary and have students chant through them again two to three times. Spend time explaining the Grammar Lesson, paying special attention to the examples. You may want to have students read the Grammar Lesson aloud, and then ask them which sentences appear to be the most important. Have the students circle those key sentences (with a colored pencil, if possible) for future reference. After this, the worksheet can be started in class or assigned as homework. The students should also begin *Activity Book!* exercises (to impart mastery of the vocabulary and paradigm).

3

Day Three: Once again, the day should start with some quick chanting of the paradigm and vocabulary. The worksheet should be either started or completed. Check students' work and have them make any necessary corrections. Grammar should be reviewed and retaught as necessary. One means of reviewing grammar can be to view the grammar video again, to ensure students understand the key grammatical concepts for that chapter. Continue with *Activity Book!* assignments (this could be done as homework or as part of the students' seatwork).

4

Day Four: Have students do a quick chanting of the paradigm and vocabulary. Next, have them complete the puzzles from the *Activity Book!* chapter. Review the video as necessary. Begin the *History Reader* after students have completed the worksheet. (**Note:** We suggest starting the *LFCA History Reader* roughly halfway through the *LFCA* textbook.)

5

Day Five: Students should take the quiz. Finish/complete the *History Reader* chapter.

A Note about
Diglot Weaves

Throughout this book, students will read "Along the Appian Way," a diglot-weave, or "spliced," adventure story that features Latin vocabulary tucked within an English-language narrative.

The diglot-weave story is an opportunity for young Latin learners to master Latin vocabulary and some other longer Latin phrases while also enjoying an exciting account of characters on an incredible journey. However, such a diglot weave will cause a clash of English and Latin grammatical rules and, as a result, there will be some inconsistencies in the rendering of Latin word endings. Additionally, students using *Latin for Children Primer A* are still in the earlier stages of their Latin studies, which means that in a diglot-weave story, they will inevitably encounter grammar that they have not yet learned. As such, we cannot display all the proper Latin endings governed by the use of Latin words in the English story. It is our experience that the dual enticement of reading an adventure and figuring out the Latin words and phrases means that the inconsistencies of the Latin inflections do not come to the attention of nor trouble young Latin learners. We have therefore adopted the following protocol for using Latin in our diglot-weave story:

- **Verbs:** Verbs are rendered with the proper person, number, and tense they would have if the story were written entirely in Latin.

- **Nouns:** Nouns appear primarily in the nominative case (except for some instances in which a noun is an object of a preposition, or when it is a possessive genitive), and are either singular or plural. We have done this so as not to introduce Latin case uses that students have not yet learned.

- **Adjectives:** Adjectives will agree with the nouns they modify.

- **Prepositions:** When a preposition is used in a prepositional phrase with a noun, we have tried to put the noun in the appropriate case (either ablative or accusative). In other instances, the context necessitates the use of an English preposition coupled with a Latin noun.

- **Adverbs:** Adverbs appear as given, since they do not vary nor decline.

- **Interjections:** Interjections appear as given, since they do not vary nor decline.

- **Infinitives:** Infinitives appear as given and sometimes take an object.

- **Pronouns:** Pronouns are almost always in the nominative case except when governed by a preposition or governed by a verb that turns the pronoun into a direct object (in which case the pronoun is rendered in the accusative case). While this last point is inconsistent with the way we display nouns, which are generally not changed into the accusative case when they are direct objects, we thought it helpful to do so with pronouns in order to familiarize students with these very common uses of the pronoun, and especially the frequent use of *is, ea, id*.

- **Conjunctions:** Conjunctions appear as given.

Along the Appian Way, Part 1

Italy, during the reign of Tiberius Julius Caesar, AD 14–37

Marcus stared down at the road beneath his feet, studying it intently.

"Did you find any yet?" asked Julia, who was now getting quite bored. "Why did I decide *dare* (___to give___) my afternoon for this silly hunt?" She kicked a rock, sending it skittering away.

Marcus moved back and forth, methodically scanning between the stones that made up the road. He didn't answer, but reviewed the map on the scroll he was holding.

"Hello? Marcus, are we rich yet? I could have stayed home if I wanted *labōrāre* (___to work___)."

Marcus looked up. "No, but I bet there's something right around the corner. This is the Appian Way, the finest road in the world! *Amō* (___I love___) this road! Remember when we found three coins all in the same day?" He tapped an area on the map. "Right here by the *silva* (___forest___)."

"Yes, yes. And we nearly got arrested for theft!" said Julia. "Remember that part of the *fābula* (___story___)?"

Marcus shook his head. "If we could even find one coin, it could buy us—"

"Wait! Wait . . ." Julia interrupted. She got quiet and listened. "Do you hear that?" The *terra* (___earth___) began to shake.

A horse suddenly galloped into view, rounding the corner from behind a line of cypress trees. Julia dove off the side of the road. Marcus froze as the rider barrelled down on him.

Grammar Lesson

Verbs: Action Words

In this first chapter, you will learn five verbs and five nouns. The first five words on your vocabulary list are verbs. **Verbs are words that show action or a state of being.** For example, in the clause "I work in the forest," which word is the action word? Well, "work," of course! The way we say "I work" in Latin is *labōrō*: so *labōrō* is a verb, a Latin action word. Sometimes verbs can show a state of being, too, like when we say, "He *is* tired." The word "is" is a kind of verb that shows a state of being (being tired), but we will teach you about verbs that show a state of being later. For now, just remember the definition of verbs as words that show action or a state of being.

Chapter 1

Grammar Lesson

Latin: Fewer Words Than English, But Many Word Endings

There are a lot of words in English, but they rarely have different endings. For example, the verb "love" stays the same whether we say "I love," "we love," or "they love." Sometimes we do add an ending, like when we say "he loves" or "we loved." In Latin, though, the verb for love (*amō*) changes its ending very often! We will learn the various endings that come with Latin verbs (and nouns) so that we can know what they mean and how to translate them. (**To translate a Latin word, by the way, means to tell what a Latin word means in English.** The translation of *amō* is "I love.") Now you know that Latin is a language of many endings, but fewer words than English!

Look at the chant chart at the beginning of the chapter. It shows you one of the most common words in Latin (the verb "love") with all its endings: the singular and the plural for present, active, and indicative—six endings in all. When we list a verb with all its endings, it's called **conjugating** a verb. **TN**

You can also see that a Latin verb such as *amō* actually contains two words in English! The word *amō* means "I love," so it contains not only the word "love," but also the word "I." The ending of the verb (*-o* in this case) tells you that it is "I" who is doing the loving. **Pronouns such as "I," "you," "he," "she," "it," "we," and "they" are all little words that tell you who is doing the action of the verb.** The ending of a Latin verb tells you which pronoun to use in English. We will study these endings next week, so don't worry too much about them now. Figure 1-1, however, shows you how the verb endings change:

> **Teacher's Note:** This is from the Latin *coniugō*, which means "join together," because when we conjugate a verb we join an ending to the verb's stem.

	Singular	Plural
1st person	**amō**: I love	**amāmus**: we love
2nd person	**amās**: you love	**amātis**: you all love
3rd person	**amat**: he, she, or it loves	**amant**: they love

Figure 1-1: **Verb endings** for *amō*

A Verb in Four Parts: The Four Principal Parts

If you look at the Memory Page, you will see that each Latin verb has four different forms (*amō, amāre, amāvī, amātum*). We call each form a **principal part**. Why? Because each part is an important form that shows us how to make other forms of the verb. It is a principal part because it is an *important* part to know. No need to worry about the other forms that come from these principal parts: you will learn those in good time. Learning the principal parts now, however, will be fun and will save you a lot of time later!

Worksheet

A. Translation

1. **amō** I love
2. **intrō** I enter
3. **dō** I give
4. **labōrō** I work
5. **fābula** story
6. **In prīncipiō erat Verbum.** In the beginning was the Word.

7. **aqua** water
8. **porta** gate
9. **nārrō** I tell
10. **silva** forest
11. **terra** earth

B. Chant

Conjugate the verb **amō**. See if you can remember how to fill in the boxes.

	Singular	Plural
1st person	**amō**	amāmus
2nd person	amās	amātis
3rd person	amat	amant

C. Grammar

1. In Latin, both _____verbs_____ and _____nouns_____ have endings.

2. Latin is a language of fewer _____words_____ but many _____endings_____ .

3. What kind of word names the action or state of being in a sentence? **A verb**

4. To _____conjugate_____ a verb is to _____list_____ all of its _____forms_____ .

D. Derivatives

On the next page we explain what a derivative is, but before you head there, in the following sentences try to figure out the derivative by circling the word that you think might come from the Latin word that is provided.

1. Aesop is famous for his (fables) / animals. (*fābula*)

2. Reward will follow hard **times** / (labor) (*labōrō*)

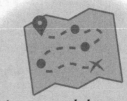

As you travel along your Latin adventure, check off your progress using the checklist that begins on page 245.

Thousands of English words come from Latin. We call these English words **derivatives** because they are derived (taken) from an original Latin word called the Latin **root**. For instance, the word "derivative" is itself a derivative. It comes from the Latin words *dē* (down from) and *rīvus* (river, stream). This means that a derivative is a word that flows down or off a river of . . . words!

A. Study

Study the following English derivatives that come from the Latin words you have learned this week:

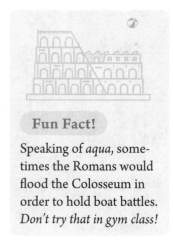

Latin	English
amō	amity, amorous, enamor, amateur
dō	donate, donation
intrō	entrance, introduce, introduction
labōrō	labor, laboratory
nārrō	narrate, narration, narrative
aqua	aquatic
fābula	fable, fabulous
porta	portable, port
silva	Pennsylvania
terra	extraterrestrial, terrain, terrarium

Fun Fact!

Speaking of *aqua*, sometimes the Romans would flood the Colosseum in order to hold boat battles. *Don't try that in gym class!*

B. Define

In a dictionary, look up one of the English derivatives from the list above and write its definition in the space below:

_____

C. Apply

1. The Latin phrase *terra firma* is still used by English speakers today. Here is an example of its use: "After being on a plane for six hours, it sure felt good to walk on *terra firma*." What do you think the phrase *terra firma* might mean? Write your answer below:

   Terra firma means "firm ground."

2. The word "Pennsylvania" is another Latin derivative. *Pennsylvania* was one of the original thirteen colonies that formed the United States. It was founded by William Penn. What do you think the word "Pennsylvania" might mean? Circle your answer below:

   a. The land of big pencils   b. The land of Penn   (c. Penn's Woods)
   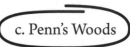

Quiz

A. Vocabulary

Latin	English
amō, amāre, amāvī, amātum	I love, to love, I loved, loved
dō, dare, dedī, datum	I give, to give, I gave, given
intrō, intrāre, intrāvī, intrātum	I enter, to enter, I entered, entered
labōrō, labōrāre, labōrāvī, labōrātum	I work, to work, I worked, worked
nārrō, nārrāre, nārrāvī, nārrātum	I tell, to tell, I told, told
aqua, aquae	water
fābula, fābulae	story
porta, portae	gate
silva, silvae	forest
terra, terrae	earth

B. Chant   Conjugate the verb *amō*.

See if you can remember how to fill in the boxes.

	Singular	Plural
1st person	**amō**	amāmus
2nd person	amās	amātis
3rd person	amat	amant

C. Grammar   Define the following words.

1. Conjugation: **The listing of all of a verb's forms or endings.**

2. Verb: **A word that shows action.**

3. List the four principal parts:

Present, Infinitive, Perfect, and Passive Participle or Supine

Along the Appian Way, Part 2

As he watched the horse galloping toward him, Marcus couldn't decide which way to jump to get out of the way. The rider pulled hard on the reins. The horse skidded and slipped as it tried to stop on the smooth rocks on the surface of the Roman *via* (_____road_____).

Julia gasped. Marcus only managed to wince and clamp his eyes shut. The horse stopped just in front of Marcus, snorting warmly in his face.

Unfortunately, the rider did not stop.

Julia watched as the rider tumbled up over the horse's neck and launched into the air over Marcus's head. The rider landed on his back with a nasty thump, his bag falling into a *fossa* (_____ditch_____), spilling several scrolls and a half-eaten loaf of bread onto the ground.

All was still again except for a soft *aura* (_____breeze_____).

Marcus and Julia quickly scrambled over to the rider to help. As Julia helped the rider to his feet, Marcus collected the scattered scrolls. He noticed the glittering gold seals that secured some scrolls.

"Are you OK?!"

"I am sooooo sorry."

The messenger looked dazed but he hastily dusted himself off. Then he turned with a scowl and grabbed his scrolls from Marcus's hands.

"I . . . I didn't mean to be in your—"

Without so much as a word, the rider swung back up on his horse. With a kick of his heels, the rider and horse disappeared down the *via* (_____road_____).

Grammar Lesson

Present-Tense Verb Endings

	Singular	Plural
1st person	**-ō**	**-mus**
2nd person	**-s**	**-tis**
3rd person	**-t**	**-nt**

Figure 2-1:
Present-tense verb endings

Worksheet

A. Translation   New and Review Vocabulary

1. **amō** I love

2. **rēgīna** queen

3. **via** road, way

4. **pātria** fatherland, country

5. **fābula** story

6. **In prīncipiō erat Verbum.** In the beginning was the Word.

7. **amātis** you all love

8. **intrant** they enter

9. **nārrās*** you tell

10. **labōrāmus*** we work

11. **dat*** he/she gives

*Note that these verb forms come from the conjugation of *nārrō*, *labōrō*, and *dō*. See the previous page. Can you conjugate these verbs in all their forms?

B. Chant   Give the present-tense verb endings and fill in the boxes.

	Singular	Plural
1st person	-ō	-mus
2nd person	-s	-tis
3rd person	-t	-nt

C. Grammar

1. The number of a verb answers the question "___How many___?"

2. Latin is a language of many ___endings___ but fewer ___words___.

3. Write the ending that fits the description below:

Description	Ending
1st person singular	-ō
3rd person plural	-nt
2nd person singular	-s

4. To conjugate a verb is to list all of its ___endings or forms___.

D. Derivatives

1. To find out about dinosaurs you must dig up a ___fossil___. (*fossa*)

2. To find out what happens next in the story, turn the ___page___. (*pāgina*)

Derivatives

A. Study

Study the English derivatives that come from the Latin words you have learned this week.

Latin	English
via	way, viaduct
fossa	fossil, fossilize
mēnsa	mesa
pāgina	page
cēna	cenacle
pātria	patriot, patriotic
aura	aroma
rēgīna	reign, regal
īnsula	insular, insulate

Fun Fact!

Insula was also the name given to a type of apartment building used in ancient Roman cities. *Insula* were usually 3 or 4 stories high and often took up a whole city block.

B. Define

In a dictionary, look up two of the English derivatives from the list above and write their definitions in the spaces below:

1. _____

2. _____

C. Apply

1. The Latin word *via* is still used by English speakers today. Here are some examples:

    "He traveled here *via* airplane."
    "Come *via* the freeway. Don't drive through the city streets."

In these sentences, *via* probably means:

    a. very   b. by way of   c. quickly

2. The Latin word *pātria* means "fatherland." In the patriotic song "My Country, 'Tis of Thee" by Samuel Francis Smith, what clue can you find that helps you understand why people often call their country their "fatherland"?

    My country, 'tis of thee,   Land of the pilgrims' pride,
    Sweet land of liberty,   From every mountainside
    Of thee I sing;   Let freedom ring!
    Land where my fathers died,

    It is the land where their fathers lived and died.

    _____

Quiz

A. New Vocabulary

Latin	English
via, viae	road, way
fossa, fossae	ditch
mēnsa, mēnsae	table
mēta, mētae	turning point, goal
pāgina, pāginae	page
cēna, cēnae	dinner
pātria, pātriae	fatherland, country
aura, aurae	breeze
rēgīna, rēgīnae	queen
īnsula, īnsulae	island

B. Review Vocabulary

Latin	English
dō, dare, dedī, datum	I give, to give, I gave, given
labōrō, labōrāre, labōrāvī, labōrātum	I work, to work, I worked, worked
aqua, aquae	water
silva, silvae	forest
terra, terrae	earth

C. Chant
Give the present-tense verb endings and fill in the boxes.

	Singular	Plural
1st person	-ō	-mus
2nd person	-s	-tis
3rd person	-t	-nt

D. Grammar
Define the following terms.

1. Number: How many people are doing the verb's action (singular or plural).

2. Person: Who is doing the verb's action (1st, 2nd, or 3rd person).

Chapter 3

Memory Page

Chapter Maxim

Arma virumque canō.*

Of arms and the man I sing. —Vergil's *Aeneid*

New Chant

First-Declension Noun—*mēnsa*

Case	Noun Job**	Singular	Plural
Nominative	SN, PrN	**mēnsa**: table	**mēnsae**: tables
Genitive	PNA	**mēnsae**: of the table	**mēnsārum**: of the tables
Dative	IO	**mēnsae**: to, for the table	**mēnsīs**: to, for the tables
Accusative	DO, OP	**mēnsam**: the table	**mēnsās**: the tables
Ablative	OP	**mēnsā**: by, with, from the table	**mēnsīs**: by, with, from the tables

Vocabulary

Latin	English
Verbs	
errō, errāre, errāvī, errātum	I wander, to wander, I wandered, wandered
stō, stāre, stetī, statum	I stand, to stand, I stood, stood
parō, parāre, parāvī, parātum	I prepare, to prepare, I prepared, prepared
spectō, spectāre, spectāvī, spectātum	I look at, to look at, I looked at, seen
sum, esse, fuī, futūrum	I am, to be, I was, about to be **TN**
Nouns	
ancilla, ancillae (f)	maidservant
glōria, glōriae (f)	glory
īra, īrae (f)	anger
unda, undae (f)	wave
fenestra, fenestrae (f)	window

Teacher's Note: The verb *sum, esse, fui, futurum* is an irregular verb, but one that is very common. You will note that the forms of its principal parts don't follow the pattern of other (regular) verbs in this list. For now, students will simply need to memorize this important verb as an irregular verb.

*Canō is a synonym of *cantō*. Both verbs mean "I sing."

**The letters in this column are abbreviations (short ways of saying something) for noun jobs that will be explained in chapter 9. Note them, but there is no need to memorize them.

Along the Appian Way, Part 3

Marcus decided that he was done getting rich for one day. He and Julia ran off to play somewhere safer.

Julia threw a rock into the ocean as a small *unda* (_____wave_____) splashed gently onto the beach. "It's a good thing you didn't hurt that scroll you borrowed. You know what our teacher, Master Balbus, would have done to you if you had ripped his map? You don't want to stir up his *īra* (_____anger_____)."

"No, I do not and I don't want to think about it," Marcus said as he tried to relax, squishing his toes into the warm sand. "*Sum* (_____I am_____) happy *stāre* (_____to stand_____) here and try to relax. Getting nearly run over by a horse is scary enough for one day, thank you."

Marcus pulled out the borrowed map of his hometown once more. He knew if he were ever to be a Roman road builder he would have to study the very best—

Wait a minute! Marcus spun the scroll around in his hands. It seemed to be stuck together and wouldn't open.

He gasped. Julia spun around *spectāre* (_____to look at_____) Marcus. "What's wrong?"

"I'm dead."

The scroll that now lay in Marcus's hand was not his teacher's scroll. The scroll in Marcus's hand had a bright golden seal!

Grammar Lesson

Noun Declensions

Do you remember what a noun is from your English grammar class? Just in case you forgot, **a noun is a word that names a person, place, thing, or sometimes an idea.** Do you remember how in the last chapter we found that verbs have all sorts of different endings? Well, nouns have a whole set of endings all their own. As we have learned, when we put together all of the different forms of a verb, we call it **conjugating** a verb. When we put together the different forms of a noun, we call it **declining** a noun. When we create a chart of a declined noun, we call that chart a **declension**.

Worksheet

A. Translation   New and Review Vocabulary

1. **errō** I wander
2. **stō** I stand
3. **parō** I prepare
4. **spectō** I look at
5. **sum** I am
6. **Arma virumque canō.** Of arms and the man I sing.
7. **fossa** ditch
8. **pātria** fatherland, country
9. **īra** anger
10. **unda** wave
11. **via** road, way

B. Chant   Fill in the endings and translate the forms of *mēnsa* given below. The first one has been done for you.

Case	Singular	Plural
Nominative	**mēns** a: table	**mēns** ae: tables
Genitive	**mēns** ae: of the table	**mēns** ārum: of the tables
Dative	**mēns** ae: to or for the table	**mēns** īs: to or for the tables
Accusative	**mēns** am: table	**mēns** as: tables
Ablative	**mēns** ā: by, with, from the table	**mēns** īs: by, with, from the tables

C. Grammar

1. A **noun** names a **person** , **place** , **thing** or **idea** .

2. Singular and **plural** are the two options for **number** .

3. Number answers the question " **How many** ?"

4. Masculine, **feminine** , and neuter are the three options for **gender** .

5. Giving all the endings for a verb is called conjugating it, whereas listing all the forms of a noun is called **declining** it.

D. Derivatives

1. Watching football on the couch can be called a **spectator** sport. (*spectō*)

2. To **defenestrate** something is to throw it out the window. (*fenestra*, preceded by *dē* for "out")

Derivatives

A. Study

Study the English derivatives that come from the Latin words you have learned this week:

Latin	English
errō	error, erroneous
stō	station, stationary, static
parō	prepare, parry, pare
spectō	spectator, spectacle, spectacular, speculate
ancilla	ancillary
glōria	glorious, glorify, glory
īra	irritate, irate, irritable
unda	undulate, inundate
fenestra	defenestrate

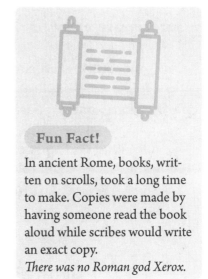

Fun Fact!

In ancient Rome, books, written on scrolls, took a long time to make. Copies were made by having someone read the book aloud while scribes would write an exact copy.
There was no Roman god Xerox.

B. Define

In a dictionary, look up three of the English derivatives from the list above and write their definitions in the spaces below:

1. _____

2. _____

3. _____

C. Apply

1. *Errāre hūmānum est.* This is a famous saying from the Roman philosopher Seneca. Can you figure out what it means? (Hint: *hūmānum* means "human.")

Give your translation here: __To err is human._____

2. "Inundate," a derivative of the Latin word *unda*, means "to flood with *waves*." The following sentence uses "inundate" and several other derivatives. Underline all the derivatives in this sentence:

The secretary was <u>inundated</u> with so much paperwork that she made <u>error</u> after <u>error</u> and became extremely <u>irritated.</u>

3. Now write your own sentence using at least two derivatives from this week's vocabulary list above.

_____

_____

A. New Vocabulary

Latin	English
errō, errāre, errāvī, errātum	I wander, to wander, I wandered, wandered
stō, stāre, stetī, statum	I stand, to stand, I stood, stood
parō, parāre, parāvī, parātum	I prepare, to prepare, I prepared, prepared
spectō, spectāre, spectāvī, spectātum	I look at, to look at, I looked at, seen
sum, esse, fuī, futūrum	I am, to be, I was, about to be
ancilla, ancillae	maidservant
glōria, glōriae	glory
īra, īrae	anger
unda, undae	wave
fenestra, fenestrae	window

B. Chant Give the chant for the declension of *mēnsa* and fill in the boxes.

Case	Noun Job	Singular	Plural
Nominative	SN, PrN	mēnsa	mēnsae
Genitive	PNA	mēnsae	mēnsārum
Dative	IO	mēnsae	mēnsīs
Accusative	DO, OP	mēnsam	mēnsās
Ablative	OP	mēnsā	mēnsīs

C. Grammar Define the following terms.

1. Noun: part of speech that names a person, place, thing, or idea

2. Declension: listing of all the forms of a noun

3. What question does the number of a noun answer? How many?

4. What are the two options for number? singular and plural

5. What are the three options for gender? masculine, feminine, and neuter

Along the Appian Way, Part 4

Marcus bit at his fingernails while he paced the floor of his house.

Julia lingered off to one side near the door. She was just a *puella* (_____girl_____) from next door and she wasn't sure this was the best time to be there.

"What am I supposed to do?!" Marcus lamented to his Mom and his *amīca* (_____friend_____).

Marcus's mother was working like a *serva* (_____slave_____) on the evening's dinner. She paused and glanced up, offering a sympathetic smile. "I'm sorry you lost the scroll, Marcus."

"I didn't lose the scroll, it was . . . it was stolen!" Marcus blurted.

His mom paused with her knife in midstroke as she was cutting the evening's vegetables. With her eyebrows raised, she looked over to Julia, whom she treated like her own *fīlia* (_____daughter_____).

Julia said, "Not exactly stolen, ma'am. More like accidentally—"

"It doesn't matter!" Marcus interrupted. "What am I supposed to do now?"

"Just relax, Marcus," his mother said. "I am sure we will be able *labōrāre* (_____to work_____) on this problem and do the right thing."

"The right thing?! And what is that?"

Grammar Lesson

More on Case

Last week we introduced you to Latin nouns, and you learned that Latin nouns have *number*, *gender*, and *case*. They can have number because a noun can be either singular or plural—there can be either one girl (*puella*) or many girls (*puellae*). Nouns can have gender because they can be either feminine, masculine, or neuter (that means that they're not masculine or feminine). A *puella* is a girl and is feminine.

Worksheet

A. Translation   New and Review Vocabulary

1. discipula **female student**
2. ancilla **maidservant**
3. domina **female master/mistress**
4. īra **anger**
5. fenestra **window**
6. Arma virumque canō. **Of arms and the man I sing.**

7. puella **girl**
8. spectō **I look at**
9. germāna **sister**
10. magistra **female teacher**
11. fēmina **woman**

B. Chant   Fill in the first-declension endings and the boxes with the missing labels.

Case	Singular	Plural
Nominative	-a	-ae
Genitive	-ae	-ārum
Dative	-ae	-īs
Accusative	-am	-ās
Ablative	-ā	-īs

C. Grammar

1. What does the case of a noun tell us?

   its role or job in a sentence

2. What are the options for case?

   nominative, genitive, dative, accusative, ablative

3. Write the present-tense verb endings.

   -ō, -s, -t, -mus, -tis, -nt

D. Derivatives

1. In chapter 3, you learned that first-declension nouns are almost always ___**feminine**___ in gender. (fēmina)

2. If someone is friendly, he or she can be called ___**amicable**___. (amīca)

Derivatives

A. Study

Study the English derivatives that come from the Latin words you have learned this week:

Latin	English
fēmina	female, feminine
fīlia	filial
germāna	germane
magistra	magistrate, magisterial
discipula	disciple, discipline
domina	dominate, dominion, domain
famula	family, familiar, familiarize*
serva	servant, servitude, service
amīca	amity, amicable

*Note that this derivative is explained in the Apply section of this worksheet.

Fun Fact!

When attacking a city, the Roman army used large machines like the ballista and onager to fire heavy stones at the enemy. They also dug under the city walls to make them collapse so they could charge in.

B. Define

In a dictionary, look up two of the English derivatives from the list above, as well as the word "family," and write their definitions in the spaces below:

1. _____

2. _____

Family: _____

C. Apply

A *famula* was a female servant or slave in a Roman household. A male servant was called a *famulus*. A household of servants or slaves was called a *familia*. We get our English word "family" from the Latin words *famula*, *famulus*, and *familia*.

When you looked up the word "family," you saw that it is used in several different ways. We can even speak of a family of Romance languages that all came from Latin (the language of the Romans). Do you know what some of the Romance languages are? Circle the languages below that you think might have come from Latin. (Hint: It will be hard for you to be wrong.)

ITALIAN   SPANISH   FRENCH

ROMANIAN   PORTUGUESE

Quiz

A. New Vocabulary

Latin	English
puella, puellae	girl
fēmina, fēminae	woman
fīlia, fīliae	daughter
germāna, germānae	sister
magistra, magistrae	female teacher
discipula, discipulae	female student
domina, dominae	female master/mistress
famula, famulae	female servant
serva, servae	female slave
amīca, amīcae	female friend

B. Review Vocabulary

Latin	English
errō, errāre, errāvī, errātum	I wander, to wander, I wandered, wandered
sum, esse, fuī, futūrum	I am, to be, I was, about to be
stō, stāre, stetī, statum	I stand, to stand, I stood, stood
īra, īrae	anger
unda, undae	wave

C. Chant Give the first-declension noun endings and fill in the boxes.

Case	Singular	Plural
Nominative	-a	-ae
Genitive	-ae	-ārum
Dative	-ae	-īs
Accusative	-am	-ās
Ablative	-ā	-īs

D. Grammar Answer the following questions.

1. What does case help us figure out? <u>It helps us figure out the noun's job in a sentence.</u>

2. What is the mnemonic sentence that helps us remember the cases? _____

<u>**N**ever **G**ive **D**avus **A**ny **A**pples.</u>

Chapter 5

Now that you have learned forty Latin words (ten words in each chapter), it is time to review them to make sure you won't forget them. Remember to practice reciting these words for 5–10 minutes every day. Try to give the English words for each Latin word on the following list. For each word that you miss, put a check in the box next to that word. Then work really hard on those checked words until you have them mastered! If you want to, write the English words by the Latin words. Remember to chant or sing the words several times every day. Review this list at least once every day this week.

VERBS

Chapter 1	Chapter 3
❑ amō I love	❑ errō I wander
❑ dō I give	❑ stō I stand
❑ intrō I enter	❑ parō I prepare
❑ labōrō I work	❑ spectō I look at
❑ nārrō I tell	❑ sum I am

NOUNS

Chapter 1	Chapter 3
❑ aqua water	❑ ancilla maidservant (f)
❑ fābula story	❑ glōria glory
❑ porta gate	❑ īra anger
❑ silva forest	❑ unda wave
❑ terra earth	❑ fenestra window

Chapter 2	Chapter 4
❑ via road, way	❑ puella girl
❑ fossa ditch	❑ fēmina woman
❑ mēnsa table	❑ germāna sister
❑ mēta turning point, goal	❑ fīlia daughter
❑ pāgina page	❑ magistra teacher (f)
❑ cēna dinner	❑ discipula student (f)
❑ pātria fatherland, country	❑ domina master (f)/mistress
❑ aura breeze	❑ famula servant (f)
❑ rēgīna queen	❑ serva slave (f)
❑ īnsula island	❑ amīca friend (f)

Along the Appian Way, Part 5

Marcus was a very sad *puer* (_____boy_____) as he sat alongside the road plucking at the tall grass. "This has got to be the second-worst day of my life."

Julia flitted from one rock to the next trying to keep her balance. "Why second worst?"

"Because, when I go before our teacher at *lūdus* (_____school_____) tomorrow and tell him that I lost his map, *that* will officially be the worst day. He won't be very happy with a *discipulus* (_____student_____) like me!"

Julia felt compelled to nod in agreement. "So, how long are we planning on waiting here?"

"As long as it takes for the rider to realize his mistake and come back here to return my scroll."

"What if the *vir* (_____man_____) doesn't come back until tomorrow? Or maybe weeks from now? What if he can't remember where it was that the accident happened? What if—"

"I don't know!" Marcus yelled, throwing up his arms. "That's why I brought you along. You're the smart one."

"Me? Why, thank you," said Julia. She rested her chin on her hand and squinted thoughtfully. "Hmmm . . . What would I do if I had lost *magister* (_____Master_____) Balbus's scroll? I'd be pretty scared. Scared enough to go to the watchmen and—"

"That's it!" Marcus blurted. "You're brilliant!" He jumped to his feet and began running. "Come on!"

Grammar Lesson

Masculine (Second-Declension) Nouns and How to Recognize Them

OK, boys, here they are—a list of many masculine words just for you. Note that they are all marked with (m). You can see why almost all of these words are masculine, such as "boy," "man," and "brother." But why in Latin is a word like "school" a masculine word and "table" a feminine word? Well, we're sorry to tell you that there isn't really a good reason for this; that's just the way that the Latin language is. Of course, when we're dealing with words for people, there usually is a good reason for a word being one gender or the other. You can see below, for example, that the last ten nouns of chapter 4 are almost exactly the same as the first ten nouns of this chapter, which you are

A. Translation New and Review Vocabulary

1. **magister** _male teacher/master_
2. **discipulus** _male student/disciple_
3. **magistra** _female teacher_
4. **discipula** _female student_
5. **discipulī** _students (plural)_
6. **Cum tacent, clāmant.** _When they are silent, they shout._

7. **servus** _male slave_
8. **famulus** _male servant_
9. **dominus** _male master_
10. **amīcus** _male friend_
11. **germānus** _brother_

B. Chant Give the declension of *lūdus* (fill in the endings and provide translations).

Case	Noun Job	Singular	Plural
Nominative	SN, PrN	lūd__us__: school*	lūd__ī__: schools
Genitive	PNA	lūd__ī__: of the school	lūd__ōrum__: of the schools
Dative	IO	lūd__ō__: to/for the school	lūd__īs__: to/for the schools
Accusative	DO, OP	lūd__um__: the school	lūd__ōs__: the schools
Ablative	OP	lūd__ō__: by/with/from the school	lūd__īs__: by/with/from the schools

*can be translated as "school," "game," or "play"

C. Grammar

1. A male teacher is called a _____**magister**_____.

2. A female student is called a _____**discipula**_____.

3. The case of a noun tells you **its role or job in the sentence (or its relationship to the other words around it)**.

4. The five cases are nominative, _____**genitive**_____, dative, _____**accusative**_____, and ablative.

D. Derivatives

1. Someone who is behaving boyishly is behaving in a _____**puerile**_____ way. (*puer*)

2. Filial behavior describes the relation between a father and a _____**son**_____. (*filius*)

A. New Vocabulary

Latin	English
puer, puerī	boy
vir, virī	man
germānus, germānī	brother
lūdus, lūdī	school, game, play
fīlius, fīliī	son
magister, magistrī	male teacher/master
discipulus, discipulī	male student/disciple
dominus, dominī	male master
famulus, famulī	male servant
servus, servī	male slave
amīcus, amīcī	male friend

B. Review Vocabulary

Latin	English
nārrō, nārrāre, nārrāvī, nārrātum	I tell, to tell, I told, told
intrō, intrāre, intrāvī, intrātum	I enter, to enter, I entered, entered
silva, -ae	forest
porta, -ae	gate
fābula, -ae	story

Chapter 6

Quiz

C. Chant   Give the declension of *lūdus* (provide endings and translations) and fill in the boxes.

Case	Noun Job	Singular	Plural
Nominative	SN, PrN	-us: school*	-ī: schools
Genitive	PNA	-ī: of the school	-ōrum: of the schools
Dative	IO	-ō: to/for the school	-īs: to/for the schools
Accusative	DO, OP	-um: the school	-ōs: the schools
Ablative	OP	-ō: by/with/from the school	-īs: by/with/from the schools

*can be translated as "school," "game," or "play"

D. Grammar   Answer the following questions.

1. What does the case of a noun help tell you?

It tells you its role in the sentence.

2. Name the five cases in order:

Nominative

Genitive

Dative

Accusative

Ablative

Along the Appian Way, Part 6

Marcus and Julia stood anxiously before a watchman, or vigiles. Marcus held out his hands as he described the size and shape of their found scroll. "It's this *magnus* (_____large_____) and it has a gold seal on it. It's marked 'secret' so we didn't open it and I hid it at home to keep it safe."

The vigiles squinted at them suspiciously. "Where did you say that you found it?"

"Along the Appian *Via* (_____Way_____)," Marcus responded.

Julia chimed in "We were there looking for lost coins that sometimes get dropped on the *via* (_____road_____). Once we found a whole—"

"Shh! He doesn't care about that," Marcus whispered.

"What did this rider look like exactly?" the *vigiles* (_____watchman_____) asked with a yawn.

"He was wearing a red toga," Marcus said. "And he had a satchel full of—"

"It was blue. And the horse he was riding was a—"

"What was blue?"

"The toga the rider was wearing was blue, not red" Julia said. "I think that was important."

"Look kids," the officer interrupted. "I don't know anything about your secret scroll and I don't know where it is supposed to go. I need *demōnstrāre* (____to point out____) that I've got more important things to worry about right now than what color cloak your make-believe friend was wearing when he nearly ran you over." The officer straightened and waved them away. "Now get out of here! I've got important work to do—my duty is *vigilāre* (_____to guard_____) the city."

Grammar Lesson

"To Be": *sum, esse*

Can you guess one of the most popular words in the Latin language? (Oops, looks like we gave it away in our subtitle . . .) You guessed it, it's *sum, esse,* the verb for "to be." You learned the meaning of this word a few weeks ago, but this week you are actually learning to conjugate it (learn and list all its forms). If you look carefully at the chart on the previous page, maybe you can see why this verb is different enough that you need to learn it separately. While the endings (in bold) usually fit the pattern, the rest of the word (what we call the **stem**) changes quite a bit. Verbs that don't follow regular patterns in Latin are called **irregular** verbs. This, then, is your first irregular verb. Since it is used so often, there is good reason to take the time to memorize it as its own chant.

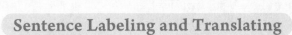
Sentence Labeling and Translating

1. **Labeling:** Now let's learn how to label the words in a sentence. The subject in a sentence is a noun (person, place, or thing) that often performs the action of the verb. Verbs are words that show action. Label the subject as *SN* for "subject noun." Label the verb with a *V*. Here's an example:

SN   V

Famula labōrat.

The servant works.

2. **Translating:** When you label a sentence, it is like making a road map for translation. Once you know each word's job, you are ready to translate. Do you remember from your English class what a sentence is? That's right, **a sentence is a group of words that makes a complete thought and includes both a subject and a verb**. When you put the two together, you have a complete sentence. Try translating the following sentences.

    SN   V
1. **Fēmina intrat.** __The woman enters.__

    SN   V
2. **Dominus stat.** __The master stands.__

    SN   V
3. **Amīcae stant.** __The friends stand.__

    SN   V
4. **Servī labōrant.** __The slaves work.__

Jewelry: *Gold aurei of the Twelve Caesars, ca. 46 BC–AD 68*

A. Translation   New and Review Vocabulary

1. **habitās** you live

2. **vigilāmus** we guard

3. **dēmōnstrō** I point out

4. **clāmātis** you all shout

5. **tardō** I delay

6. **Cum tacent, clāmant.** When they are silent, they shout.

7. **hortus** garden

8. **lupī** (nom.) wolves

9. **ancillārum** (gen.) of the maidservants

10. **fenestra** window

11. **parō** I prepare

B. Chant   Give the missing present-tense endings and translations for *sum* and label the unlabeled boxes.

	Singular		Plural	
1st person	sum	: I am	**sumus**:	we are
2nd person	**es**:	you are	estis	: you all are
3rd person	est	: he, she, it is	**sunt**:	they are

C. Grammar

1. The subject of a sentence is usually a noun.

2. Label and translate the following sentences:

SN   V
Socius vigilat. The associate (or ally) guards.

SN   V
Lupī habitant. The wolves live.

D. Derivatives

1. An associate is someone with whom one is allied.
   (*socius* preceded by *a* for "to or toward")

2. To demonstrate something is to point it out. (*dēmōnstrō*)

Quiz

A. New Vocabulary

Latin	English
vigilō, vigilāre, vigilāvī, vigilātum	I guard, to guard, I guarded, guarded
clāmō, clāmāre, clāmāvī, clāmātum	I shout, to shout, I shouted, shouted
tardō, tardāre, tardāvī, tardātum	I delay, to delay, I delayed, delayed
habitō, habitāre, habitāvī, habitātum	I live, to live, I lived, lived
dēmōnstrō, dēmōnstrāre, dēmōnstrāvī, dēmōnstrātum	I point out, to point out, I pointed out, pointed out
hortus, -ī	garden
lupus, -ī	wolf
socius, -ī	ally, associate
aquārius, -ī	water carrier

B. Review Vocabulary

Latin	English
errō, errāre, errāvī, errātum	I wander, to wander, I wandered, wandered
stō, stāre, stetī, statum	I stand, to stand, I stood, stood
parō, parāre, parāvī, parātum	I prepare, to prepare, I prepared, prepared
spectō, spectāre, spectāvī, spectātum	I look at, to look at, I looked at, seen
fenestra, -ae	window

C. Chant Fill in the missing labels and the present-tense endings and translations for *sum*.

	Singular	Plural
1st person	sum: I am	sumus: we are
2nd person	es: you are	estis: you all are
3rd person	est: he, she, it is	sunt: they are

D. Grammar Label and translate the following sentences.

    SN   V

1. **Aquārius labōrat.** The water carrier works. _____

    SN   V

2. **Servī clāmant.** The slaves shout. _____

Roman Coins

The Roman Republic began around 510 BC, when the Romans rebelled against the ruling kings and set up a government ruled by elected senators. The Republic lasted for over 450 years, until it was replaced by the solitary rule of one emperor, in part by Julius Caesar in 49 BC and completely by Augustus in 27 BC. With Augustus, the Roman Empire began and lasted until Rome was sacked by German invaders in AD 476. Millions of Roman coins were minted throughout the duration of both the Roman Republic and the Roman Empire.

Facts about Roman Coins:

- They were almost always stamped with the image of an emperor or famous Roman ruler.
- Roman coins were made of gold, silver, or bronze.
- They were usually made to celebrate people, gods, ideals, and important events.
- In addition to the image of an emperor or famous Roman ruler, Roman coins featured various symbols, such as snakes, images of the gods, flowers, wreaths, and weapons.
- They showed the views, beliefs, and leaders of the times, much like our coins today do.

- Silver coins were very popular but became debased (lost value) over time.
- Abbreviations for words were used on Roman coins because of the limited surface area available.
- The word "coin" comes from the Latin *cuneus*, which means "wedge," because wedge-shaped tools (dies) were used to stamp the coins.

Roman coins are still being unearthed today and can easily be purchased over the Internet! You can collect your own Roman coins—have your parent or teacher search the Internet with you.

Along the Appian Way, Part 7

As the morning sun crested the rocks on the horizon, Marcus's mother called, "Marcus! Are you awake?"

Marcus was still in bed. "I am" he replied, but he moaned as he held his stomach. "Oh, I don't feel well. I don't think I can go to the *lūdus* (_____school_____) today. I don't feel well enough even *ambulāre* (_____to walk_____)."

Marcus's mom paused as she walked past his bedroll on her way to pick vegetables from their *hortus* (_____garden_____). She stifled her smile. "Do you think it was the oysters we had last night or is it the scroll that you lost that makes you so sick today?"

"Mom! I really do feel sick. I need *auxilium* (_____help_____) just to get up. I think going to school today would not be—"

"I should not have *dēmōnstrāre* (_____to point out_____) to you that you can't run from this forever, Marcus," his mother said gently. "Sooner or later, you must be brave enough *stāre* (_____to stand_____) before your *magister* (_____teacher_____) and tell him everything. You have to do the right thing. I'm sure he will understand."

"Do you think so?" Marcus asked.

Marcus's mom shrugged. "I really don't know. Even if *magister* (_____Master_____) Balbus doesn't understand, it is the right thing to do, and I know that you can be brave."

Marcus sat up in bed. He thought about it. "You're right! *Tardō* (_____I delay_____) too long." With a smile, he jumped up and threw on his clothes.

Grammar Lesson

Neuter Nouns

So far we've talked about the masculine and feminine genders, and this week we have one more to talk about. The last one is the **neuter** gender. Think of neuter, if you will, as a "neutral" gender. The English word "neuter" comes from the Latin *neuter*, meaning "neither"; that's because neuter nouns are neither masculine nor feminine. In English, most nouns are neuter, since it is only people or animals that we regard as masculine or feminine. In Latin, however, only a small number of words are neuter. That's because so many nouns in Latin are masculine (such as *lūdī*, "schools") or feminine (such as *mēnsae*, "tables"). Before we move on, take a careful look at the chart at the beginning

A. Translation

1. **necō** I kill
2. **caelum** sky
3. **pugnāmus** we fight
4. **puerī** boys
5. **auxiliī** of help
6. **Dīvidē et rēgnā.** Divide and rule.

7. **servum** slave
8. **mandant** they entrust
9. **dominus** master
10. **exempla** examples
11. **oppugnās** you attack

B. Chant
Fill in the missing forms and translations for *dōnum* and fill in the missing labels.

Case	Singular	Plural
Nominative	dōnum: gift	dōna: gifts
Genitive	**dōnī**: of the gift	dōnōrum: of the gifts
Dative	dōnō: to/for the gift	**dōnīs**: to/for the gifts
Accusative	**dōnum**: the gift	dōna: the gifts
Ablative	dōnō: by/with/from the gift	**dōnīs**: by/with/from the gift

C. Grammar

1. In Latin, the _____ **case** _____ of the noun allows us to need fewer of those little words called

   _____ **prepositions** _____, such as "to," "for," or "of."

2. According to the _____ **neuter** _____ rule, words with the _____ **neuter** _____ gender will

   always have the same endings in the nominative and _____ **accusative** _____ cases, and the neuter
   nominative and accusative plural always end in a short *a*.

D. Derivatives

1. A person with a _____ **mandate** _____ has been entrusted to do something. (*mandō*)

2. Many people make a _____ **donation** _____ to their favorite charity at Christmas. (*dōnum*)

Derivatives

A. Study

Study the English derivatives that come from the Latin words you have learned this week:

Latin	English
pugnō TN	pugnacious, pugilist
oppugnō	repugnant
ambulō	amble, ambulance, ambulatory, perambulator
mandō	mandate, mandatory
aedificium	edifice, edify
caelum	celestial
auxilium	auxiliary
exemplum	example, exemplary
dōnum	donate, donation, donor

Fun Fact!

Students would write by using a metal pen called a *stylus* to scratch on panels of wood covered in wax. The flat "eraser" on the end let them smooth out mistakes in the wax.

B. Define

In a dictionary, look up three of the English derivatives from the list above and write their definitions in the spaces below:

1. _____

2. _____

3. _____

> Teacher's Note: The Latin word *pugil* (related to *pugno*) means "boxer." The Latin word *repugno* is related to *oppugno*. *Repugno* means "to oppose" or "resist."

C. Apply

Let's look at the derivatives of another Latin word. Surely you have seen an *ambulance* go screaming by with its lights flashing. But how can the word "ambulance" be related to *ambulō*, which means "I walk"? Well, there was a time before the invention of cars when wounded soldiers were carried off battlefields on stretchers and carts that were pulled by other people. They were called by the French name *hôpital ambulant* or "walking hospital." Even though ambulances now are powered by motors instead of humans, we still call them ambulances. The word "amble," which means "to walk at an easy or careless pace," is also from the Latin *ambulō*. Other words derived from *ambulō* include *perambulator*, which is another name for a baby carriage (usually with four wheels), and *ambulatory*. If someone is ambulatory, he or she is capable of walking. A six-month-old baby is not ambulatory.

Write a brief paragraph below using one of the *ambulō* derivatives and at least two other derivatives from this week's vocabulary list above.

_____

_____

_____

A. New Vocabulary

Latin	English
pugnō, pugnāre, pugnāvī, pugnātum	I fight, to fight, I fought, fought
oppugnō, oppugnāre, oppugnāvī, oppugnātum	I attack, to attack, I attacked, attacked
necō, necāre, necāvī, necātum	I kill, to kill, I killed, killed
ambulō, ambulāre, ambulāvī, ambulātum	I walk, to walk, I walked, walked
mandō, mandāre, mandāvī, mandātum	I entrust, to entrust, I entrusted, entrusted
aedificium, -ī	building
caelum, -ī	sky
auxilium, -ī	help
exemplum, -ī	example
dōnum, -ī	gift

B. Review Vocabulary

Latin	English
puer, -ī	boy
vir, virī	man
germānus, -ī	brother

C. Chant Give the chant and translations for *dōnum* and fill in the boxes.

Case	Singular	Plural
Nominative	dōnum: gift	dōna: gifts
Genitive	dōnī: of the gift	dōnōrum: of the gifts
Dative	dōnō: to/for the gift	dōnīs: to/for the gifts
Accusative	dōnum: the gift	dōna: the gifts
Ablative	dōnō: by/with/from the gift	dōnīs: by/with/from the gifts

D. Grammar Give the definition or answer the question for each item below.

1. What kind of word do the cases of Latin frequently include when translated into English?

   prepositions

2. Give two examples of the kind of word mentioned above.

   Answers will vary, but examples include to, for, of, by, with, from, etc.

3. Give the neuter rule. Neuter nouns always have the same forms in the nominative and

   the accusative (and the plural forms of the neuter nominative and accusative will
   always end with *a*).

Roman Villa

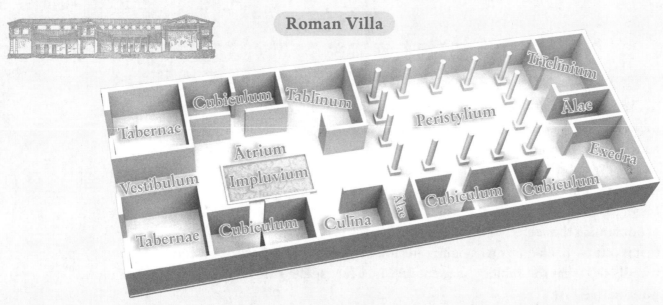

Along the Appian Way, Part 8

Marcus and Julia walked toward the *lūdus* (_____ school _____). The scroll with the golden seal was tucked under Marcus's arm. "You know, the more I thought about it, *magister* (_____ Master _____) Balbus might actually be thrilled that I lost his lousy old scroll," Marcus said. "I mean, when he sees this new scroll and the gold seal on the *pāgina* (_____ page _____) . . . who knows what's inside?"

"Maybe it's a treasure map!" Julia blurted.

"Yes! Or maybe it's a royal decree from Caesar himself. Who knows?"

Julia hopped and skipped and then walked backward in front of Marcus. She looked him straight in the eye. "Do you think he might give you a *praemium* (_____ reward _____) or a *dōnum* (_____ gift _____) for the new scroll?"

A new grin appeared on Marcus's face. "Maybe!"

"What?! You lost my scroll?!" Balbus's face was bright red and he threw his hands up to the *caelum* (_____ sky _____). "Why did I chose *mandāre* (_____ to entrust _____) the scroll to a *puer* (_____ boy _____)?! Why must this be my *fātum* (_____ fate _____)?!"

Marcus felt quite ashamed, but held out the other scroll. "But I have this other one instead. Can you imagine what might be inside of it?"

"It won't be of any *auxilium* (_____ help _____) to me!" the professor spat, smacking it aside. "You will pay me for the lost scroll! Do you understand?!"

Grammar Lesson

Noun Jobs! The Nominative Case Is Used for the Subject

You may have noticed that there is something different about the table on the previous page. Can you tell what the change is? A new column has been added: the column that tells you what **noun job** a case can fill. A noun's case ending can substitute for a preposition, but it can also tell you how the noun fits in with the other words in the sentence. It tells you what the noun is doing there; that is, it tells you what the noun's job is. Do you remember talking about finding the subject of a sentence in your English grammar class? Well, that is one particular job that a noun can have in a sentence. **In Latin, you can usually tell what the subject of a sentence is, because the subject is in the nominative case.**

Grammar Lesson

A linking verb is like an equal sign (=) in math.

The Nominative Case Is Also Used for the Predicate Nominative

All of the other major noun jobs are listed in the new noun-job column as well, but there is only one other noun job that we are going to worry about today: the **predicate nominative**.* Can you guess what case a predicate nominative is in? That's right, it's in the *nominative* case. Predicate nominatives are always used with **linking verbs**—verbs that link the subject with another word. So far, the only linking verb that you know is *sum, esse*. If you see that verb, you know that it may be followed in the sentence with a predicate nominative. **Predicate nominatives rename the subject.** Here is an example: **TN**

SN LV PrN
Jūlia est puella.

Another name for Jūlia is *puella* (girl)!

*The predicate nominative can also be called the **predicate noun**.

Painting: *The Women of Rome Gathering at the Capitol* by Pieter Isaacsz, ca. 1600–1602

A. Translation   New and Review Vocabulary

Turn the singular nouns into plural nouns, then translate all of the words.

1. **beneficium** <u>beneficia: gifts</u>

7. **hortus** <u>hortī: gardens</u>

2. **gaudium** <u>gaudia: joys</u>

8. **amīca** <u>amīcae: friends</u>

3. **mēnsa** <u>mēnsae: tables</u>

9. **socius** <u>sociī: associates</u>

4. **frūmentum** <u>frūmenta: grains</u>

10. **fātum** <u>fāta: fates</u>

5. **lupus** <u>lupī: wolves</u>

11. **collum** <u>colla: necks</u>

6. **Dīvidē et rēgnā.** <u>Divide and rule.</u>

B. Chant   Give the second-declension neuter endings and fill in the boxes.

Case	Singular	Plural
Nominative	-um	-a
Genitive	-ī	-ōrum
Dative	-ō	-īs
Accusative	-um	-a
Ablative	-ō	-īs

C. Grammar

1. The subject noun and predicate <u>noun or nominative</u> are the two noun jobs that will always be seen in the nominative case.

2. The <u>predicate</u> <u>noun or nominative</u> renames the subject.

D. Derivatives

1. <u>Horticulture</u> is the growing of garden plants. (*hortus*)

2. *Equine* means "like a horse"; <u>lupine</u> means "like a wolf." (*lupus*)

A. New Vocabulary

Latin	English
fātum, -ī	fate
forum, -ī	public square
oppidum, -ī	town
perīculum, -ī	danger
frūmentum, -ī	grain
praemium, -ī	reward
astrum, -ī	star
beneficium, -ī	benefit, gift
gaudium, -ī	joy
collum, -ī	neck

B. Review Vocabulary

Latin	English
hortus, -ī	garden
lupus, -ī	wolf
socius, -ī	ally, associate
aquārius, -ī	water carrier
dēmōnstrō, dēmōnstrāre, dēmōnstrāvī, dēmōnstrātum	I point out, to point out, I pointed out, pointed out

C. Chant Give the second-declension neuter endings and fill in the boxes.

Case	Singular	Plural
Nominative	-um	-a
Genitive	-ī	-ōrum
Dative	-ō	-īs
Accusative	-um	-a
Ablative	-ō	-īs

D. Grammar Give the definition or answer the question for each item below.

1. What two noun jobs are always in the nominative case?

   subject and predicate nominative

2. Predicate nominative:

   A noun that appears after a linking verb and a subject, and renames the subject.

Latin Today: Professions

Many professions (kinds of jobs or careers) use words that come from Latin. Therefore, studying Latin will help you more easily understand the special words used by the professions listed below.

Law

Jobs: lawyers, judges, legal secretaries, paralegals

Usage: Many legal words are **loan words** that come directly from the Latin. The word "legal" comes from the Latin word for law: *lēx, lēgis*.

Examples: judge, court, testimony, defendant, prosecutor, sentence

Loan Words: *mea culpa, habeās corpus, stāre dēcīsis, ā fortiōrī, sub silentiō, nunc prō tunc*

Medicine

Jobs: doctors, dentists, chiropractors, physical therapists, nurses, technicians, medical insurance and service professionals

Usage: The names of parts of the body and of diseases usually come from Latin. The word "medicine" comes from the Latin word *medicina*, which means "remedy."

Examples: ovum, pelvis, retina, saliva, etc.

Chapter **10**

Another four weeks of study and you have learned another forty words. As you did during the last review week, make sure you have these words mastered. Put a check next to each word you don't know. Then write all the words you need to master on the next page, and review those words as much as you need to in order to master them. Remember to look at the words while chanting them.

Chapter 6

- ❏ **puer** boy
- ❏ **germānus** brother
- ❏ **fīlius** son
- ❏ **magister** male teacher/master
- ❏ **discipulus** male student/disciple
- ❏ **dominus** male master
- ❏ **famulus** male servant
- ❏ **lūdus** school, game, play
- ❏ **servus** male slave
- ❏ **amīcus** male friend
- ❏ **vir** man

Chapter 8

- ❏ **pugnō** I fight
- ❏ **oppugnō** I attack
- ❏ **necō** I kill
- ❏ **ambulō** I walk
- ❏ **mandō** I entrust
- ❏ **aedificium** building
- ❏ **caelum** sky
- ❏ **auxilium** help
- ❏ **exemplum** example
- ❏ **dōnum** gift

Chapter 7

- ❏ **vigilō** I guard
- ❏ **clāmō** I shout
- ❏ **tardō** I delay
- ❏ **habitō** I live
- ❏ **dēmōnstrō** I point out
- ❏ **lupus** wolf
- ❏ **socius** ally
- ❏ **aquārius** water carrier
- ❏ **hortus** garden

Chapter 9

- ❏ **fātum** fate
- ❏ **forum** public square
- ❏ **oppidum** town
- ❏ **perīculum** danger
- ❏ **frūmentum** grain
- ❏ **praemium** reward
- ❏ **astrum** star
- ❏ **beneficium** benefit, gift
- ❏ **gaudium** joy
- ❏ **collum** neck

Grammar Review First- and Second-Declension Nouns and Review of Forms/Chants

Fill out the boxes below, showing all forms of the noun *mēnsa, mēnsae* and the noun *lūdus, lūdī*. If you don't know some of these words, you need to go back and study some more. Chant using your eyes and voice. Turn to chapters 3 and 6 to check your work.

First Declension, Feminine

Case	Singular	Plural
Nominative	**mēnsa**: table	**mēnsae**: tables
Genitive	**mēnsae**: of the table	mēnsārum: of the tables
Dative	**mēnsae**: to, for the table	**mēnsīs**: to, for the tables
Accusative	mēnsam: the table	**mēnsās**: the tables
Ablative	**mēnsā**: by, with, from the table	mēnsīs: by, with, from the tables

Second Declension, Masculine

Case	Singular	Plural
Nominative	**lūdus**: school	**lūdī**: schools
Genitive	**lūdī**: of the school	**lūdōrum**: of the schools
Dative	lūdō: to, for the school	lūdīs: to, for the schools
Accusative	lūdum: school	**lūdōs**: schools
Ablative	**lūdō**: by, with, from the school	lūdīs: by, with, from the schools

Sentence Building: Study the sentences in the box, then translate the sentences below.

Magister vigilat. *The teacher guards/keeps watch.*	**Dominus clāmat.** *The master shouts.*	**Germānus pugnat.** *The brother fights.*
Fīlia habitat. *The daughter lives.*	**Servī dēmōnstrant.** *The slaves point out.*	**Amīca ambulat.** *The friend walks.*

Lupus vigilat.
The wolf guards/keeps watch.

Oppidum oppugnat.
The town attacks.

Famulus necat.
The servant kills.

Socius mandat.
The ally entrusts.

Puerī ambulant.
The boys walk.

Discipulae errant.
The students wander.

Grammar Review (continued)

Complete the table for *sum* (I am): Check your work by turning to chapter 7.

	Singular	Plural
1st person	sum	sumus
2nd person	es	estis
3rd person	est	sunt

Sentence Labeling (Diagramming) Study the the sentences in the first box, then label the sentences below.

Do you remember what *SN* stands for? It is the **subject noun**. Whenever a noun (a person, place, or thing) does the action in a sentence, it is called the subject or subject noun.

Do you remember what *V* stands for? It is the **verb**. The word in a sentence that is an action word is a verb. Look at the sentence below:

SN   V

The teacher watches.

SN V	SN V	SN V
Magister vigilat.	**Dominī clāmant.**	**Germānī pugnant.**
SN V	SN V	SN V
Fīlius habitat.	**Servus dēmōnstrat.**	**Amīcus ambulat.**

SN V	SN V	SN V
Lupī vigilant.	**Oppidum oppugnat.**	**Famulus necat.**
SN V	SN V	SN V
Socius mandat.	**Puerī ambulant.**	**Discipulae errant.**

The Noun Job of the Nominative Case

Whenever we find a noun in the nominative case (always the first case listed), it will do the job of a subject noun. Look at the following sentence:

Lupus vigilat.

Do you see that *lupus* is in the nominative case (check your chart if you need to)? That is how we know it is the subject. *Lupus* is doing the action of *vigilat*—The wolf guards/keeps watch!

Second-Declension Neuter Nouns: *dōnum, dōnī*

Second Declension, Neuter

Case	Singular	Plural
Nominative	**dōnum**: gift	**dōna**: gifts
Genitive	**dōnī**: of the gift	**dōnōrum**: of the gifts
Dative	dōnō: to, for the gift	dōnīs: to, for the gifts
Accusative	dōnum: the gift	**dōna**: the gifts
Ablative	**dōnō**: by, with, from the gift	dōnīs: by, with, from the gifts

Do you remember the neuter rule?

Any noun that is neuter will have the same endings in both the nominative and the accusative cases. If we have *dōnum* in the nominative (singular), then we will have *dōnum* in the accusative (singular). If we have *dōna* in the nominative (plural), then we will have *dōna* in the accusative (plural)!

Noun Jobs   Nominative Case, Predicate Nominative

When a **subject noun** (SN) is renamed as something else, we use a **linking verb** (LV) (such as "is") to link the subject to another noun. Look at the sentences below:

SN LV PrN
Julia is a girl.

SN LV PrN
Jūlia* est puella.

SN LV PrN
Julia = girl

Julia is renamed as a girl. We could also say that Julia is "linked" with the word "girl." If we were doing math, we would use an = sign to show that Julia is "linked" to *girl* (Julia = girl). Since the word "girl" is another noun that simply renames our subject (Julia), it is also in the nominative case just as the subject is (*Jūlia* and *puella* are both in the nominative case). We call it the **predicate nominative** (**PrN**). The word "predicate" (*praedicō, praedicāre*) means "to make known." When we say "Julia is a girl," we make it known that Julia . . . is a girl!

---

*Jūlia/Iūlia can be translated as either Julia or Julie in English.

Chapter 10

Translating and Labeling

Study the first box, then label and translate the sentences in the second box.

    SN LV PrN
Mārcus est amīcus.
Marcus is a friend.

      SN   LV PrN
Germānus est magister.

The brother is a teacher.

    SN LV PrN
Fīliī sunt discipulī.
The sons are students.

     SN LV PrN
Amīcī sunt germānī.

The friends are brothers.

      SN   LV PrN
Dominus est socius.
The master is an associate.

    SN LV PrN
Jūlia est amīca.

Julia is a friend.

    SN LV PrN
Servus est fīlius.
The servant is a son.

     SN   LV   PrN
Amīcae sunt discipulae.

The friends are students.

Latin Today: Professions (cont.)

    Many professions (kinds of jobs or careers) use words that come from Latin. Therefore, studying Latin will help you more easily understand the special words used by the professions listed below.

Science

Jobs: scientists of all kinds, such as biologists, physicists, geologists, chemists, etc.

Usage: The names of plants, animals, minerals, chemicals, elements, and rocks are usually from Latin. The word "science" comes from the Latin word for knowledge: *scientia, -ae.*

Examples: animal, phylum, solar, aquatic

Music

Jobs: musicians, composers, conductors, vocalists, choirs

Usage: The various names for the elements of music are often from Latin (sometimes through Greek). The word "music" comes from the Greek into the Latin as *mūsica, -ae.*

Examples: tempo, rhythm, meter, note, signature, etc.

Along the Appian Way, Part 9

Marcus was up to his knees in mud. Surrounding him were some of the largest hogs he had ever seen. He felt *parvus* (_____small_____) compared to them and twice as dirty.

Marcus was doing his best to pick up extra chores and odd jobs around the *oppidum* (_____town_____) in order to earn the money he needed to pay back his *magister* (_____teacher_____). Marcus had been running around helping this farmer ever since he got out of *lūdus* (_____school_____), and his legs and back ached. The farmer paid him a *parvus* (_____small_____) wage, but Marcus needed the money.

It took quite a bit of effort to hold the slop containers away from the hungry hogs. Bumped and jostled about, Marcus tried *ambulāre* (_____to walk_____) his way through the muck toward the trough.

"Coming through!" He sniffed at the *aura* (_____breeze_____). "Ugh! I don't know which smells worse, you guys or what you eat. Look out!"

He was suddenly and rudely knocked over by a *magna* (_____large_____), hairy sow. The pig feed went flying. It scattered on the muddy *terra* (_____earth_____), which didn't seem to bother the hogs.

Unfortunately, Marcus had lost his balance in the accident. He stood up now, gasping for breath. His face was covered in dripping mud.

"Is this my *fātum* (_____fate_____)?" he cried out.

Grammar Lesson

Adjectives

We've talked a bit about nouns and verbs so far, but now it's time to bring up a third part of speech, the **adjective**. Take a look at the chart at the beginning of the chapter and you'll see that those endings look awfully familiar! That's because they're just like the noun endings that you've already learned. So why are adjective endings so much like nouns? Nouns and adjectives go together like bread and butter, like peanut butter and jelly, like hot dogs and mustard. **Adjectives, you see, describe or modify nouns.** That is, they tell you more about them. If you were to say, for example, "the tiny ball," the word "ball" is a noun and the word "tiny" is an adjective telling you what kind of

A. Translation

1. **dubitō** I doubt

2. **cōgitāmus** we think

3. **magnus** large, great

4. **errās** you wander

5. **dubius** doubtful

6. **Cōgitō ergō sum.** I think, therefore I am.

7. **parat** he/she prepares

8. **fenestra** window

9. **mūtātis** you all change

10. **vērus** true

11. **falsus** false

B. Chant
Fill in the box below with the missing adjective case endings.

	Singular			Plural		
	Masculine	Feminine	Neuter	Masculine	Feminine	Neuter
Nominative	-us	-a	-um	-ī	-ae	-a
Genitive	-ī	-ae	-ī	-ōrum	-ārum	-ōrum
Dative	-ō	-ae	-ō	-īs	-īs	-īs
Accusative	-um	-am	-um	-ōs	-ās	-a
Ablative	-ō	-ā	-ō	-īs	-īs	-īs

C. Grammar

1. The three adjective questions are: What ____kind____ ? ____Which____ one?

and ____How____ ____many____ ?

2. Adjectives must agree with the nouns they modify in ____gender____ ,

____number____ , and ____case____ .

D. Derivatives

1. Most artists are very ____creative____ . (*creō*)

2. Something that is ____dubious____ is doubtful. (*dubius*)

Derivatives

A. Study

Study the English derivatives that come from the Latin words you have learned this week:

Latin	English
creō	create, creative, creation
explōrō	explore, exploration, explorer, exploratory
cōgitō	cogitate, cogitation
mūtō	mutate, mutation, mutant
dubitō	doubt, indubitable
magnus	magnify, magnitude
parvus	parvovirus
vērus	very, verify, verity
falsus	false, falsify, falsehood, falsity
dubius	doubt, doubtful, dubious

Fun Fact!

Favorite pets among the ancient Romans included dogs, birds, and occasionally monkeys. There is also artwork showing kids being pulled in carts drawn by goats or geese. *Which of these pets would you prefer?*

B. Define

In a dictionary, look up two of the English derivatives from the list above and write their definitions in the spaces below:

1. _____

2. _____

C. Apply

1. From the Latin word *explōrō* are derived some English words that closely resemble it, including "explore," "exploration," "explorer," and "exploratory." *Exploratory* surgery may involve a doctor or surgeon looking for something, such as cancer, in a person's body. Here is an interesting fact to consider: The Latin word *explōrō* actually comes from two Latin words: *ex*, meaning "out or out of," and *plōrō*, meaning "I cry out, wail, lament." Some scholars think that a hunting cry once used to signal the start of a hunt is the basis of the word. Now when you want to go exploring, you can think of it as a kind of hunt.

Write a sentence using at least one of the derivatives of *explōrō* that we have discussed here:

_____

2. A famous French philosopher named René Descartes (ren-AY day-KART) thought that if you wanted to prove the existence of anything, you had better start by proving the existence of yourself. He decided that if he was thinking about whether or not he existed, or even doubting whether he existed, that meant that someone must be doing the thinking, and that person or being must exist! He recorded his insight using two Latin phrases. Can you translate Descartes's Latin phrases into English? (Hint: *Ergō* means "therefore.")

a. **Cōgitō ergō sum.** I think, therefore I am.   b. **Dubitō ergō sum.** I doubt, therefore I am.

A. New Vocabulary

Latin	English
creō, creāre, creāvī, creātum	I create, to create, I created, created
explōrō, explōrāre, explōrāvī, explōrātum	I explore, to explore, I explored, explored
cōgitō, cōgitāre, cōgitāvī, cōgitātum	I think, to think, I thought, thought
mūtō, mūtāre, mūtāvī, mūtātum	I change, to change, I changed, changed
dubitō, dubitāre, dubitāvī, dubitātum	I doubt, to doubt, I doubted, doubted
magnus, -a, -um	large, great
parvus, -a, -um	small
vērus, -a, -um	true
falsus, -a, -um	false
dubius, -a, -um	doubtful

B. Review Vocabulary

Latin	English
spectō, spectāre, spectāvī, spectātum	I look at, to look at, I looked at, seen
sum, esse, fuī, futūrum	I am, to be, I was, about to be
ancilla, -ae	maidservant
glōria, -ae	glory

C. Chant Give the adjective endings and fill in all the boxes.

	Singular			Plural		
	Masculine	Feminine	Neuter	Masculine	Feminine	Neuter
Nominative	-us	-a	-um	-ī	-ae	-a
Genitive	-ī	-ae	-ī	-ōrum	-ārum	-ōrum
Dative	-ō	-ae	-ō	-īs	-īs	-īs
Accusative	-um	-am	-um	-ōs	-ās	-a
Ablative	-ō	-ā	-ō	-īs	-īs	-īs

D. Grammar Answer the questions below.

1. What are the three adjective questions?

   What kind? Which one? How many?

2. Adjectives must agree with the nouns they modify in what three characteristics?

   gender, number, and case

Choose a Latin Name

Some Latin names are still used today. In fact, your name might even be a Latin name! Take a look at the list of common Latin names below. Many of them are quite strange to our ears, aren't they?

Male Names: Gāius, Lūcius, Mārcus, Pūblius, Quīntus, Titus, Tiberius, Sextus, Aulus, Decimus
Female Names: Gāia, Lūcia, Mārca, Pūblia, Quīnta, Tita, Tiberia, Sexta, Aula, Decima

Choose a Latin name from the list above or create a Latin version of your own name by selecting a Latin ending and adding it to your name.

Example: David + *-ius* = Davidius.

Boys				Girls			
-us	-imus	-entius	-āvius	-a	-ima	-entia	-āvia
-oris	-ius	-rius	-icius	-oris	-ia	-ria	-icia

Your Latin name will be: _____

Along the Appian Way, Part 10

Marcus was on the roof of an *antīquum* (＿＿＿＿old＿＿＿＿), two-story *aedificium* (＿＿building＿＿). With a *parvus* (＿＿＿small＿＿＿) hammer he was prying up several broken roof tiles. He looked up and glanced at the setting sun.

As one of the old tiles split and broke free, Marcus's foot slipped. He began sliding down the roof, sending several new tiles skittering along with him. He desperately grabbed at anything and everything. Fortunately, Marcus's hand found the edge of a secure row of tiles. He gripped the tiles tightly and jerked to a stop, one foot dangling over the edge of the roof. Phew! He was out of *perīculum* (＿＿＿danger＿＿＿)!

The loose tiles and one of his sandals continued their slide, flipping through the air and smashing on the ground below and on some sacks of *frūmentum* (＿＿＿grain＿＿＿).

Marcus caught his breath. "I hope I don't have to pay for those tiles—that would make me *miser* (＿＿miserable＿＿)!"

Gingerly, he climbed back up onto his feet and slowly made his way back up the roof.

Marcus shook his head. "It's going to take years before I can pay for that scroll." He crouched back down and began prying at another cracked tile. "And it wasn't even my fault."

Grammar Lesson

Predicate Adjectives

Remember two weeks ago when we learned about how linking verbs like *sum, esse* can tie together two different nouns? Well, we can also use linking verbs to tie together the subject with an adjective. We would call that adjective, you guessed it, the **predicate adjective**. For example:

Vir est bonus.
The man is good.

The subject here is *vir* and the adjective *bonus* is the **predicate adjective**.

Worksheet

A. Translation

1. **bonus** good
2. **nōtus** known
3. **serēnus** calm, bright, clear
4. **īrātus** angry
5. **miser** miserable
6. **Cōgitō ergō sum.** I think, therefore I am.
7. **laetus** happy
8. **amīca** female friend
9. **antīquus** old
10. **fīlia** daughter
11. **germāna** sister

B. Chant

Give the declension of the adjective *magnus, -a, -um* and fill in the boxes.

	Singular			Plural		
	Masculine	Feminine	Neuter	Masculine	Feminine	Neuter
Nominative	magnus	magna	magnum	magnī	magnae	magna
Genitive	magnī	magnae	magnī	magnōrum	magnārum	magnōrum
Dative	magnō	magnae	magnō	magnīs	magnīs	magnīs
Accusative	magnum	magnam	magnum	magnōs	magnās	magna
Ablative	magnō	magnā	magnō	magnīs	magnīs	magnīs

C. Grammar

1. When a linking verb is used to tie an adjective to the subject, we call that adjective a

   predicate adjective .

2. Label and translate each of the sentences below:

   SN V
   Vir intrat.
   The man enters.

   SN LV PrN
   Vir est magister.
   The man is a teacher.

   SN LV PrA
   Virī sunt bonī.
   The men are good.

D. Derivatives

1. A serene person is very calm. (*serēnus*)

2. A very old piece of furniture is called an antique . (*antīquus*)

89   Chapter 12

Derivatives

A. Study

Study the English derivatives that come from the Latin words you have learned this week:

Latin	English
bonus	bonus, bon voyage
malus	malfunction, malcontent
nōtus	note, notice, notation, notification
ignōtus	ignore, ignorant
novus	novel, novelty, novice
antīquus	antiquity, antique, antiquated, antiquarian
serēnus	serene, serenity, serenade
īrātus	irritate, irritated, irate, irascible
laetus	Laetare Sunday (4th Sunday in Lent)
miser	misery, miserable, commiserate, miser

Fun Fact!

Roman soldiers often had to march for hours a day carrying weapons, armor, water, cooking supplies, and other provisions, which would total more than 50 pounds.

B. Define

In a dictionary, look up two of the English derivatives from the list above and write their definitions in the spaces below:

1. _____

2. _____

C. Apply

There are several other Latin words that are related to *malus* and have *mal* at their root. All of these Latin words describe something "bad" and also give us some additional English words. You won't have to look up the definitions for these English derivatives because they mean the same thing as the Latin word!

Latin Word	Definition	Derivative
malitia	hatred	malice
malignus	wicked	malignant
malefactor	evildoer	malefactor
malevolentia	ill will	malevolence

You may have heard people talking about *malignant* or *benign* tumors. As you might have guessed, a *malignant* tumor is the bad kind, which contains cancer. A *benign* tumor, on the other hand, is a harmless tumor. The word "benign" comes from the Latin word *benignus*, which means "kind or friendly."

In the space below, list several other English words that have *mal* in them. Remember, they might be "bad" words.

Answers will vary. Some examples include malediction, malicious, malfeasance, etc.

A. New Vocabulary

Latin	English
bonus, -a, um	good
malus, -a, -um	bad
nōtus, -a, -um	known
ignōtus, -a, -um	unknown
novus, -a, -um	new
antīquus, -a, -um	old
serēnus, -a, -um	calm, bright, clear
īrātus, -a, -um	angry
laetus, -a, -um	happy
miser, misera, miserum	miserable

B. Chant Give the declension of the adjective *magnus* and fill in the boxes.

	Singular			Plural		
	Masculine	Feminine	Neuter	Masculine	Feminine	Neuter
Nominative	magnus	magna	magnum	magnī	magnae	magna
Genitive	magnī	magnae	magnī	magnōrum	magnārum	magnōrum
Dative	magnō	magnae	magnō	magnīs	magnīs	magnīs
Accusative	magnum	magnam	magnum	magnōs	magnās	magna
Ablative	magnō	magnā	magnō	magnīs	magnīs	magnīs

Quiz

C. Grammar Give the definition or answer the question of each item below.

1. Predicate adjective:

An adjective in the predicate of the sentence that the linking verb ties to the subject

2. Label and translate each of the following sentences.

SN V	SN LV PrA	SN LV PrA
Puella clāmat.	**Lupus est magnus.**	**Verba** (words) **sunt falsa.**
The girl shouts.	The wolf is large.	The words are false.

The Constellations

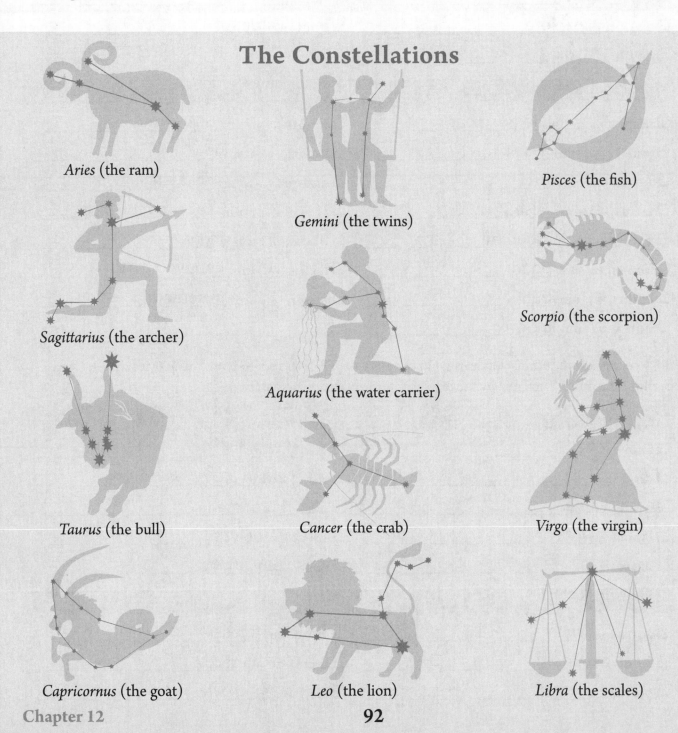

Aries (the ram)

Gemini (the twins)

Pisces (the fish)

Sagittarius (the archer)

Aquarius (the water carrier)

Scorpio (the scorpion)

Taurus (the bull)

Cancer (the crab)

Virgo (the virgin)

Capricornus (the goat)

Leo (the lion)

Libra (the scales)

Chapter 13

Well, you have learned another twenty words in the last two chapters. We, of course, want to make sure that you know them all well—and that means it is time to review. Since you've finished your first twelve chapters, we want you to review all the new words you have learned since you started the book, a total of 100 words! By now you should know our routine, so let's get to work. We will start with the words you learned in chapters 11 and 12.

VERBS

❑ creō __I create__

❑ explōrō __I explore__

❑ cōgitō __I think__

❑ mūtō __I change__

❑ dubitō __I doubt__

ADJECTIVES

❑ magnus, -a, -um __large, great__

❑ parvus, -a, -um __small__

❑ vērus, -a, -um __true__

❑ falsus, -a, -um __false__

❑ dubius, -a, -um __doubtful__

❑ bonus, -a, -um __good__

❑ malus, -a, -um __bad__

❑ nōtus -a, -um __known__

❑ ignōtus, -a, -um __unknown__

❑ novus, -a, -um __new__

❑ antīquus, -a, -um __old, ancient__

❑ serēnus, -a, -um __calm, bright, clear__

❑ īrātus, -a, -um __angry__

❑ laetus, -a, -um __happy__

❑ miser, -a, -um __miserable__

Now review the words you learned in chapters 1–4. Remember to put a check by each word you cannot remember. Then review those words until you have them mastered.

VERBS

❑ amō __I love__

❑ dō __I give__

❑ intrō __I enter__

❑ labōrō __I work__

❑ nārrō __I tell__

❑ errō __I wander__

❑ stō __I stand__

❑ parō __I prepare__

❑ spectō __I look at__

❑ sum __I am__

NOUNS

❑ aqua, -ae __water__

❑ fābula, -ae __story__

❑ porta, -ae __gate__

❑ silva, -ae __forest__

❑ terra, -ae __earth__

❑ via, -ae __road, way__

NOUNS

❏ fossa, -ae ditch	❏ unda, -ae wave
❏ mēnsa, -ae table	❏ fenestra, -ae window
❏ mēta, -ae turning point, goal	❏ puella, -ae girl
❏ pāgina, -ae page	❏ fēmina, -ae woman
❏ cēna, -ae dinner	❏ germāna, -ae sister
❏ pātria, -ae fatherland, country	❏ fīlia, -ae daughter
❏ aura, -ae breeze	❏ magistra, -ae teacher (f)
❏ rēgīna, -ae queen	❏ discipula, -ae student (f)
❏ īnsula, -ae island	❏ domina, -ae master (f)/mistress
❏ ancilla, -ae maidservant (f)	❏ famula, -ae servant (f)
❏ glōria, -ae glory	❏ serva, -ae slave (f)
❏ īra, -ae anger	❏ amīca, -ae friend (f)

Now review the words from chapters 6–9.

VERBS

❏ vigilō I guard	❏ pugnō I fight
❏ clāmō I shout	❏ oppugnō I attack
❏ tardō I delay	❏ necō I kill
❏ habitō I live	❏ ambulō I walk
❏ dēmōnstrō I point out	❏ mandō I entrust

NOUNS

❏ puer, -ī boy	❏ amīcus, -ī friend
❏ vir, virī man	❏ lūdus, -ī school
❏ germānus, -ī brother	❏ hortus, -ī garden
❏ fīlius, -ī son	❏ lupus, -ī wolf
❏ magister, -ī teacher	❏ socius, -ī associate
❏ discipulus, -ī student	❏ aquārius, -ī water carrier
❏ dominus, -ī master	❏ aedificium, -ī building
❏ famulus, -ī servant	❏ caelum, -ī sky
❏ servus, -ī slave	❏ auxilium, -ī help

NOUNS

- exemplum, -ī   example
- dōnum, -ī   gift
- fātum, -ī   fate
- forum, -ī   public square
- oppidum, -ī   town
- perīculum, -ī   danger

- frūmentum, -ī   grain
- praemium, -ī   reward
- astrum, -ī   star
- beneficium, -ī   benefit, gift
- gaudium, -ī   joy
- collum, -ī   neck

Derivative Study

Remember, derivatives are English words that come from Latin words. Let's study some derivatives from Latin words you learned in chapters 11–12.

Verbs:

creō . . . . create, creative, creation
explōrō . . . . exploration, explorer, exploratory
cōgitō . . . . cogitate (to think), cogitation (deep thought)
mūtō . . . . mutate, mutation, mutable, mutant, immutable (unchangeable)
dubitō . . . . doubt, indubitable (without doubt)

Adjectives:

magnus . . . . magnify, magnitude
parvus . . . . parvovirus (small virus), parvule
vērus . . . . very, verify, verity (state of being true or real)
falsus . . . . falsehood, falsity, falsify (to prove false)
dubius . . . . doubtful, dubious
bonus . . . . bonus (something in addition to what you expected), *bon voyage* ("good voyage" or "good trip" in French)
malus . . . . malice (desire to cause pain or harm), malfunction
nōtus . . . . notice, notable, note, notorious, notation
ignōtus . . . . ignore, ignorant
novus . . . . novel, novelty (something new or unusual)
antīquus . . . . antiquity, antique, antiquated, antiquarian
serēnus . . . . serene, serenity
īrātus . . . . irritate, irritated, irate, irascible
laetus . . . . Laetare Sunday (fourth Sunday in Lent)
miser . . . . misery, miserable, commiserate (to feel or express sympathy)

Review of Grammar

Grammar is a word that you have used a good bit since you started studying Latin. Do you know where the word "grammar" comes from? It comes from the Greek word for "letter": *gramma*. The Romans borrowed this word from the Greeks, and grammar came to mean the study of different kinds of words (such as nouns, verbs, adjectives), their endings, and how they are placed in a sentence. You have learned some valuable grammar in the last twelve chapters. Let's review it to make sure you have mastered it. For each section, you may need to go back to a chapter to find the correct answers or to check your work.

Chapters 1–2 Grammar

1. Say the chant for *amō, amās, amat* . . .

2. Write out this chant (all six words): **amō**, ___amās___ , ___amat___ ,

   ___amāmus___ , ___amātis___ , ___amant___

3. What is a conjugation? ___A list showing a verb together with its endings.___
   Write the answer, then check chapter 1 to make sure your answer is right.

4. What is a verb? ___A verb names an action or state of being in a sentence.___

Chapters 3–4 Grammar

5. What are the endings for verbs? Do you remember the chant that begins with *-ō, -s, -t* . . .? Say the

   chant and then write out the six endings: *-ō, -s, -t,* ___-mus___ , ___-tis___ ,

   ___-nt___ .

6. Do you remember that verbs have number? A verb's number refers to whether it is singular or

   ___plural___ .

   Put an *S* above the singular verbs and a *P* under those that are plural.

	S		S
We love.	*She loves.*	*They love.*	*I love.*
P		P	

7. Now do the same in Latin:

S			S
Amō.	*Amāmus.*	*Amant.*	*Amat.*
	P	P	

8. Verbs also have person. They have three persons. Do you remember them? The first person is *I love* (*amō*) or *we love* (*amāmus*). Remember, the first person can be singular or plural! What is the second person for *amō* in both the singular and plural?

   ___amās, amātis___

9. What is the third person for *amō* in both the singular and plural?

   ___amat, amant___

10. Do you remember the endings for *mēnsa, -ae* (table)? It is a first-declension noun. Try to chant the endings, then write them out:

mēnsa, mēnsae, _____**mēnsae**_____ , _____**mēnsam**_____ , _____**mēnsā**_____ .

11. Nouns also have gender. They can be masculine, feminine, or _____**neuter**_____ .

12. Finally, nouns also have case. A noun's case tells what job that noun does (noun job). There are five cases, which you have memorized by the sentence *Never Give Davus Any Apples*. Can you write out the names of these five cases?

N is for nominative. G is for _____**genitive**_____ . D is for _____**dative**_____ .

A is for _____**accusative**_____ . A is for _____**ablative**_____ .

Chapter 6 Grammar

13. Do you remember the endings for *lūdus, lūdī* (school)? Try to chant the endings, then write them

out: *lūdus, lūdī,* _____**lūdō**_____ , _____**lūdum**_____ , _____**lūdō**_____ .

What gender is *lūdus, lūdī*? _____**masculine**_____

14. What is the gender of *mēnsa, mēnsae* (from chapter 3)? _____**feminine**_____

Chapter 7 Grammar

15. You learned the irregular verb *sum* (I am) in chapter 7. Can you chant all six forms of this verb? Try to, and then write out the six forms:

sum, es, _____**est**_____ , _____**sumus**_____ , _____**estis**_____ , _____**sunt**_____ .

16. Give the Latin word for the following:

he is _____**est**_____ , we are _____**sumus**_____ , they are _____**sunt**_____ .

17. Do you remember how to label a subject and verb? Subjects are labeled with *SN* for subject noun. Verbs are labeled with a *V*. Label the following four sentences:

| SN | V | | SN | V | | SN | V | | SN | V |
| The servants work. | | **Famulae labōrant.** | | The girl enters. | | **Puella intrat.** |

18. What is a sentence? A sentence is a group of words that makes a complete thought and includes both a subject and a verb. Try to translate the following Latin sentences:

Fēmina intrat. __The woman enters._____

Dominus spectat. _____ The master looks. _____

Oppida oppugnant. _____ The towns attack. _____

Chapters 8–9 Grammar

19. Neuter nouns in the second declension are very much like masculine nouns except in the nominative and accusative cases.
    Masculine nouns have the case endings of: -us, -ī, -ō, -um, -ō; -ī, -ōrum, -īs, -ōs, -īs.
    Neuter nouns have the case endings of: <u>-um</u>, -ī, -ō, <u>-um</u>, -ō; <u>-a</u>, -ōrum, -īs, <u>-a</u>, -īs.
    The neuter endings that are the same are underlined.
    Can you chant both the masculine and neuter endings correctly?

20. What are the noun jobs for each of the five noun cases? Check chapter 9 for answers.

    Nominative: subject (**SN**), predicate nominative (**PrN**)

    Genitive: possessive noun adjective (**PNA**)

    Dative: indirect object (IO)

    Accusative: direct object (DO), object of the preposition (OP)

    Ablative: object of the preposition (OP)

21. Do you remember what a _predicate nominative_ is? It is a noun that renames the subject of a sentence. In the sentence below, _puella_ is another name for _Jūlia_ (Julia is a girl). The predicate nominative is linked to the subject by a linking verb—such as _est_. Here is an example in Latin:

    Jūlia est puella. The _PrN_ stands for predicate nominative.

Chapters 11–12 Grammar

22. Can you remember all the endings for nouns of the first and second declensions? Can you chant _all_ these endings? If needed, you can review the endings on page 77.

23. What do adjectives do? Do you remember the three questions adjectives ask?

    What kind? Which one? _____ How many? _____? Check your answer by reviewing chapter 11.

24. In Latin, adjectives and nouns agree with one another. This means they have the same gender, number, and case, such as _discipulus bonus_ (good male student) and _discipula bona_ (good female student).

25. Do you remember your sentence patterns?
    Pattern A: SN V
    Pattern B: SN LV PrN
    Pattern C: SN LV PrA
    If you are not sure what these patterns are, review sentence patterns in chapter 12.

Chant Review

Have you mastered all your tables or boxes (*tabulae*)? Now is the time to show that you have mastered them all, or finish the job of mastering them. After you have filled out each box, sing or chant it until you can do it three times without looking. If there is a box you can't fill out, circle it so you know to keep working on that one until it is mastered! If you need help, the chapter number is listed after the title of the table.

Title (ch.3) **First-Declension Noun**

Case	Singular	Plural
Nominative	**mēnsa**	mēnsae
Genitive	**mēnsae**	mēnsārum
Dative	mēnsae	mēnsīs
Accusative	mēnsam	mēnsās
Ablative	mēnsā	mēnsīs

Title (ch.4) **First-Declension Noun Endings**

Case	Singular	Plural
Nominative	-a	-ae
Genitive	-ae	-ārum
Dative	-ae	-īs
Accusative	-am	-ās
Ablative	-ā	-īs

Title (ch.7) **Second-Declension Noun Endings**

Case	Singular	Plural
Nominative	-us	-ī
Genitive	-ī	-orum
Dative	-ō	-īs
Accusative	-um	-ōs
Ablative	-ō	-īs

Title (ch.7) **Sum (I am) Chant**

	Singular	Plural
1st person	**sum**	**sumus**
2nd person	es	estis
3rd person	est	sunt

Title (ch.9) **Second-Declension Neuter Noun Endings**

Case	Singular	Plural
Nominative	-um	-a
Genitive	-ī	-ōrum
Dative	-ō	-īs
Accusative	-um	-a
Ablative	-ō	-īs

Chapter 13

Review

Noun Jobs

Do you remember that each noun case (nominative, genitive, dative, accusative, ablative) has its own job? Can you list them? Try it out in the table below. See chapter 9 for help.

Case	Noun Job	Abbreviation
Nominative	Subject , Predicate Nominative	SN, PrN
Genitive	Possessive Noun Adjective	PNA
Dative	Indirect Object	IO
Accusative	Direct Object, Object of the Preposition	DO, OP
Ablative	Object of the Preposition	OP

Now that you have reviewed the noun jobs, see if you can properly translate the different cases of *mēnsa*. If you need help, see chapter 3.

Case	Singular	Plural
Nominative	**mēnsa:** table	mēnsae: tables
Genitive	**mēnsae:** of the table	mēnsārum: of the tables
Dative	mēnsae: to the table	mēnsīs: to the tables
Accusative	mēnsam: table	mēnsās: tables
Ablative	mēnsā: by, with, from the table	mēnsīs: by, with, from the tables

Person

Finally, review what *person* means by looking at the section entitled "Person" in chapter 2. What do we mean by "first person," "second person," and "third person?"

The *first person* means "I" or "we."

The *second person* means   you or you (as in you all—plural)   .

The *third person* means   he/she/it or they   .

Remember, each person can be either singular or plural. "I" is singular, and "we" is plural, but they are both in the first person.

Along the Appian Way, Part 11

Marcus was dirty, tired, and quite hungry. He was slowly making his way home alone in the dark along the Appian *Via* (_____Way_____). He felt a bit scared since it wasn't unheard of for there to be robbers, or worse yet, hungry animals out on the *via* (_____road_____) at night.

Marcus had to stifle a few tears. Nothing was going right. The whole accident with the messenger wasn't fair. Then there was the mix-up with the scrolls . . . and now all the work he had to do for *magister* (_____Master_____) Balbus. Marcus wouldn't have wished all this on his worst enemy.

Something rustled up ahead.

Marcus froze. It was dark, making it hard *vidēre* (_____to see_____). He quickly looked around for a weapon.

All he could find was a small stick *tenēre* (_____to hold_____). Marcus was now holding it forward like it was a sword. He tried to hide behind it, hoping he could wish away whatever angry beast had found him.

"*Iubeō/Jubeō* (_____I order_____) you to show yourself!" he shouted, trying to sound brave.

"I thought it would be you," a rather perky voice said.

Marcus peeked through his clenched eyes at the speaker. He saw a *parva puella* (_____small girl_____), not a beast.

It was Julia. She had brought Marcus a basketful of food.

"Here's some *cēna* (_____dinner_____) for you, and some *aqua* (_____water_____). How was the work? Was any of it fun?" Julia asked.

Marcus couldn't answer. His mouth was stuffed with the chicken leg he was devouring.

Grammar Lesson

Videō and the Second Conjugation

Remember that when we list together all the forms that a verb can take, we call that **conjugating** a verb. In the same way, when we list the forms of a noun or an adjective, we say that we are **declining** it. Now, remember how nouns have different patterns of declension, called the first and second declensions, which have different endings and, especially, different vowels near their ends? For example, the first declension has endings that mostly have an *a* in them

A. Translation

1. **pugnō** I fight

2. **teneō** I hold

3. **augēs** you increase

4. **necās** you kill

5. **incola** settler

6. **Vēnī, vīdī, vīcī.** I came, I saw, I conquered.

7. **habēmus** we have

8. **mandātis** you all entrust

9. **iubet** he/she orders

10. **nautae** (nom.) sailors, the sailors

11. **ager** field

B. Chant   Give the conjugation of *videō*.

	Singular	Plural
1st person	videō	vidēmus
2nd person	vidēs	vidētis
3rd person	videt	vident

C. Grammar

1. To _____decline_____ a noun is to list all the endings of that noun.

2. To _____conjugate_____ a verb is to list all the endings of that verb.

D. Derivatives

1. He wore thick glasses because he had poor _____vision_____. (*videō*)

2. _____Agriculture_____ is the art and science of growing crops in the fields. (*ager, agricola*)

Derivatives

A. Study

Study the English derivatives that come from the Latin words you have learned this week:

Latin	English
videō	video, vision, visionary, evident
teneō	tenacious, tenacity, tenant, tenet, tenure
habeō	habit, habituate
augeō	augment, augmentation
ager	agriculture
poēta	poet, poetry, poetic
agricola	agriculture, agricultural
nauta	nautical

Fun Fact!

Many Roman buildings featured overlapping roof tiles called *tegula* and *imbrex*. These tiles were typically made from fired clay, and when properly used, they were waterproof. *Have you ever seen a tile roof on a modern home?*

B. Define

In a dictionary, look up two of the English derivatives from the list above and write their definitions in the spaces below:

1. _____

2. _____

C. Apply

Although the words *habeō* and *teneō* have similar meanings—*habeō* means "I have" and *teneō* means "I hold"—they are still different. To hold on to something means more than just having it. That's why a lot of the English words that are derived from the word *teneō* have to do with holding on to something with strength and determination. That's where words such as "tenacious" and "tenacity" come in. To be *tenacious* is "to be persistent, to hold on to something against difficult odds."

Example: "The small band of soldiers was *tenacious* as they defended their camp against a much larger group of attackers."

From *habeō* we get the word "habit." A *habit* is a pattern of behavior that each of us "has," you might say. The Latin word can refer to what you carry and wear, such as "I have a coat on," or "You have a hat on." A nun's or a monk's *habit* (the kind of clothing a nun or a monk wears) also comes from *habeō*.

We can all see that our word "video" comes from the Latin word *videō*! Can you think of any other English words that have the words "video" or "vision" in them? Hint: What machine do the letters *TV* stand for?

television, videography, envision, visual
_____

A. New Vocabulary

Latin	English
videō, vidēre, vīdī, vīsum	I see, to see, I saw, seen
teneō, tenēre, tenuī, tentum	I hold, to hold, I held, held
habeō, habēre, habuī, habitum	I have, to have, I had, had
iubeō, iubēre, iussī, iussum	I order, to order, I ordered, ordered
augeō, augēre, auxī, auctum	I increase, to increase, I increased, increased
agricola, -ae	farmer
nauta, -ae	sailor
poēta, -ae	poet
incola, -ae	settler
ager, agrī	field

B. Review Vocabulary

Latin	English
pugnō, pugnāre, pugnāvī, pugnātum	I fight, to fight, I fought, fought
oppugnō, oppugnāre, oppugnāvī, oppugnātum	I attack, to attack, I attacked, attacked
necō, necāre, necāvī, necātum	I kill, to kill, I killed, killed
ambulō, ambulāre, ambulāvī, ambulātum	I walk, to walk, I walked, walked

C. Chant   Conjugate *videō* and fill in the boxes.

	Singular	Plural
1st person	videō	vidēmus
2nd person	vidēs	vidētis
3rd person	videt	vident

D. Grammar   Give the definition or answer the question at each item below.

1. Conjugation: The listing of all the forms of a verb.

2. Declension: The listing of all the forms of a noun.

3. Name the first-declension masculine exceptions from this week's list.

poēta, agricola, incola, nauta

Latin Today: Professions (cont.)

Art

Jobs: painters, sculptors, historians of art, architects, poets, writers, actors, directors

Usage: Various words for art tools and concepts come from Latin. The word "art" comes from the Latin word for art: *ars, artis*.

Examples: canvas, paint, sculptor, pencil, texture, perspective

Literature

Jobs: teachers, professors, readers, writers, journalists, critics, novelists, poets, essayists

Usage: Many literary terms come from Latin. The word "literature" comes from the Latin word *litterae*, which literally means "letters"!

Examples: text, novel, verse, romance, satire, interpretation, chapter, page, character, action, development, resolution, climax

Chapter Story

Along the Appian Way, Part 12

Marcus and Julia sat in the warm, *serēnus* (_____bright_____) sunshine along the beachfront. They enjoyed the *ventus* (_____wind_____) on their faces coming in from the sea.

"Maybe someone else saw the messenger passing through the *oppidum* (_____town_____)," Julia said. "Maybe they know what direction he went."

"It's not likely anyone will remember now," Marcus said. "But I suppose it's all we have to go on." Marcus fingered the gold seal on the scroll. He really wanted to pull it off. It wouldn't likely be that hard to break. For all the *malus* (_____bad_____) trouble he had been put through because of the scroll, he now had a burning desire to know what was on the inside of it.

Julia watched Marcus carefully.

"I wouldn't do it."

"Wouldn't do what?" Marcus asked.

"I wouldn't open it."

"Why not?!" Marcus surprised himself at how *īrātus* (_____angry_____) he suddenly felt. "You know how long I'm going to have *labōrāre* (_____to work_____) to pay back the lost scroll?! I think I have a right to know what's inside this thing."

"Go ahead then," Julia said. She turned her gaze back out to sea. She was thinking about riding an *equus* (_____horse_____) on the sand . . . and her *animus* (_____mind_____) was calm.

Marcus quickly put his thumb up to the seal, ready to break it . . . but he paused and began *dubitāre* (_____to doubt_____) that it was wise to break the seal. Eventually his hand relaxed. "I guess I'll open it some other time."

They both sat in silence.

Grammar Lesson

PATTERN A: <u>SN V</u>   SN   V
             PatA   **Vir intrat.**
                            The man enters.

PATTERN B: <u>SN LV PrN</u>   SN LV   PrN
             PatB   **Vir est magister.**
                            The man is a teacher.

Worksheet

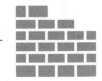

A. Translation

1. **campī** <u>level spaces</u>
2. **cibus** <u>food</u>
3. **ventōrum** <u>of the winds</u>
4. **equīs** <u>to the horses</u>
5. **oppidum** <u>town</u>
6. **Vēnī, vīdī, vīcī.** <u>I came, I saw, I conquered.</u>

7. **frūmenta** (nom.) <u>grains</u>
8. **perīculum** <u>danger</u>
9. **ferus** <u>wild animal</u>
10. **murī** (nom.) <u>walls</u>

B. Chant   Write down the Pattern A and Pattern B chants.

Pattern "A" has a simple form.
It's made with verb and a subject noun.
SN-V! SN-V!
Pattern "A" has a simple form!

Pattern "B" is a pattern of "B"eing.
Two nouns surround a small LV.
SN-LV-PrN! SN-LV-PrN!
Pattern "B" is a pattern of "B"eing!

C. Grammar

1. What are the two kinds of verbs?

   <u>action verbs and linking verbs</u>

2. Which kind of verb will be found in a Pattern A sentence?

   <u>an action verb</u>

3. Which type of verb will be found in a Pattern B sentence?

   <u>a linking verb</u>

D. Derivatives

1. An <u>equestrian</u> event is one that involves riding horses. (*equus*)

2. To <u>animate</u> means "to bring to life." (*animus*)

Derivatives

A. Study

Study the English derivatives that come from the Latin words you have learned this week:

Latin	English
animus	animus, animate, animated, animator, animation, inanimate
campus	camp, campus, encamp
annus	annual, biannual, triannual, annuity
mūrus	mural
ventus	vent
equus	equestrian, equine
ferus	feral, ferocious
fluvius	fluvial

Fun Fact!

To decorate nicer houses, the Romans didn't hang pictures or put up wallpaper. Instead they painted directly on the walls, often while the plaster walls were still damp. *Don't try this at home!*

B. Define

In a dictionary, look up two of the English derivatives from the list above and write their definitions in the spaces below:

1. _____

2. _____

C. Apply

Do you enjoy watching a good *animated* movie? Can you guess the Latin word from which the English word "animated" is derived? If you said *animus*, you're exactly right. In addition to meaning "mind," *animus* can also be translated as "spirit" or "soul." To *animate* something can mean to bring it to life—to give it a spirit. Cartoons and *animated* movies, sometimes simply called "animation," bring the drawings or computer-generated graphics "to life." An *animator* is someone who creates characters and makes them move and speak. An object that is not alive—such as a rock—is *inanimate*. It is an *inanimate* object. If someone is acting or speaking in a lively, even loud, manner, we can say that he or she is *animated*. **Example:** "The angry and *animated* customer shouted at the store manager."

Even the word *animus* itself has come into English (we call this a "loan word"). In English, "animus" means "a strong dislike, disposition, or temper."
Example: "With irritation and *animus* the customer demanded a refund from the store manager."

Can you guess what kind of living thing gets its name from *animus*? Hint: An *equus* falls into this category.

animal
_____

A. New Vocabulary

Latin	English
animus, -ī	mind
campus, -ī	level space, plain, field
annus, -ī	year
mūrus, -ī	wall
cibus, -ī	food
ventus, -ī	wind
equus, -ī	horse
ferus, -ī	wild animal
fluvius, -ī	river

B. Review Vocabulary

Latin	English
praemium, -ī	reward
astrum, -ī	star
beneficium, -ī	benefit, gift
gaudium, -ī	joy
collum, -ī	neck

C. Chant   Give the Pattern A and Pattern B chants.

Pattern "A" has a simple form.
It's made with verb and a subject noun.
SN-V! SN-V!
Pattern "A" has a simple form!

Pattern "B" is a pattern of "B"eing.
Two nouns surround a small LV
SN-LV-PrN! SN-LV-PrN!
Pattern "B" is a pattern of "B"eing!

D. Grammar

1. What are the two kinds of verbs?

   action verbs and linking verbs

2. Which kind of verb will be found in a Pattern A sentence?

   an action verb

3. Which type of verb will be found in a Pattern B sentence?

   a linking verb

Latin Today: Military Names

Many military words come from Latin, including the word "military" itself, which comes from the Latin word for "soldier," which is *miles, militaris*. The following is a list of other military words that are related to Latin.

- **Army:** from *arma* (arms) and *armāta* (armada). The verb *armō, armāre* means "to arm."

- **Navy:** from *nāvis* (ship)

- **Submarine:** from *sub* (under) and *mare* (sea)

- **Fort:** from *fortis* (strong)

- **Camp:** from *campus* (field)

Chapter Story

Along the Appian Way, Part 13

The *forum* (__public square__) offered many colorful choices of *cibus*
(__food__) and common objects for the home. It was a fun place in which *errāre*
(__to wander__). Marcus and Julia talked with an *antīquus* (__old__)
fishmonger. He had all sorts of fish, both dead and alive.

Marcus hesitated and then pulled out the scroll from a bag.

"*Habeō* (__I have__) a valuable scroll," Marcus said.

He showed the seller the fine seal of *aurum* (__gold__) that bound the scroll
shut. The fish seller shook his head and pointed elsewhere.

Julia talked to the next seller, who was surrounded by many wheels of cheese, some *magnī*
(__large__) and some *parvī* (__small__). The seller did not want any
colloquium (__conversation__) with an *ignōta puella* (__unknown girl__) and quickly
shrugged and turned away, showing a large, pale block of cheese to an inquiring customer.

Marcus talked to two *fēminae* (__women__) who were displaying folds of
beautifully colored cloth. They talked briefly, but both shook their heads. One of them patted
Marcus on the head before he turned away.

"I don't know if anyone saw the rider or they just don't remember," Marcus sighed.

"I know," Julia twisted her lip. "There are too many people that come through here and he just
wouldn't stand out."

"Unless he tried to run you over," Marcus said without a smile. Julia snorted a short laugh.

"Well, there are a few more sellers we haven't talked to yet. I guess we may as well keep trying."

Marcus and Julia pushed between the nearest crowd of people and continued *errāre*
(__to wander__) and search for any sign of the messenger.

Grammar Lesson

The Imperfect Tense

Up until now, the only tense that we've been working with is the present
tense. In fact, we haven't talked about tense at all! So what is tense? Remember this definition: **Tense is time**. Chant that definition over and over. Tense
tells you *when* something happens. All verbs have tense in Latin. So add tense

Worksheet

A. Translation

1. **arat** <u>he/she plows</u>
2. **novus** <u>new</u>
3. **ignōtus** <u>unknown</u>
4. **vītō** <u>I avoid</u>
5. **malus** <u>bad</u>
6. **Ars longa, vīta brevis.** <u>Art is long, life is brief.</u>

7. **flāmus** <u>we blow</u>
8. **aurum** <u>gold</u>
9. **argentō** (dat.) <u>to the silver</u>
10. **bracchia** <u>arms</u>
11. **colloquium** <u>conversation</u>

B. Chant

Give the imperfect-tense verb endings and label the other blank boxes.

	Singular	Plural
1st person	-bam	-bāmus
2nd person	-bās	-bātis
3rd person	-bat	-bant

C. Grammar

Parse, label, and translate the following sentences. Be sure to include the sentence pattern as well.

   SN   V

1. **Nauta nāvigat.** SN / V PatA   The sailor sails.
Nom/S/M 3/S/Pr

  SN LV PrN

2. **Vir est nauta.** SN LV / PrN PatB The man is a sailor.
Nom/S/M↑N/S/M
    3/S/Pr

D. Derivatives

1. Land that is arable is able to be <u>plowed</u>. (*arō*)

2. Without your <u>vocal</u> cords, you wouldn't have a voice. (*vocō*)

A. Study

Study the English derivatives that come from the Latin words you have learned this week:

Latin	English
arō	arable
nāvigō	navigate, navigation, navigator, circumnavigate
flō	inflate, inflation, flatulence
vocō	voice, vocal, vocalize, vocation, invoke, evoke, provoke, revoke
aurum	auric
argentum	Argentina, argentiferous
bracchium	brace, embrace, bracelet
colloquium	colloquial
cōnsilium	counsel, conciliatory

Fun Fact!

Olive trees were very important to Romans. The oil made from olives was used to cook, to light lamps, and to make soap. Olive branches were also used for the winner's crown in the Olympics.

B. Define

In a dictionary, look up two of the English derivatives from the list above and write their definitions in the spaces below:

1. _____

2. _____

C. Apply

The Latin word for voice is *vōx*, which is closely related to *vocō*. After all, we use our voice—*vōx*—when we call—*vocō*—someone. There are lots of English words that are derived from the Latin *vōx* and *vocō*. For instance, anything *vocal* refers to the use of our voice. To *invoke* means "to call in" (did you know that *in* in Latin means "in"?), in the sense of calling in aid and help. Therefore, to *invoke* can mean "to pray for help." **Example:** "In the midst of the storm, the sailors *invoked* God's help."

To *evoke* means "to call out" (*ē, ex* means "out" in Latin) in the sense of calling out feelings, memories, or other things. **Example:** "The song *evoked* a memory of days past."

To *provoke* means "to call forth" (*prō* means "before, in front of") in the sense of challenging, angering, or enraging someone. **Example:** "He slapped him, *provoking* him into a fight."

To *revoke* means "to call back or again" (*rē* means "back") in the sense of taking back or canceling. **Example:** "The store *revoked* its double-your-money-back guarantee."

The word "vocation" refers to one's "calling" or work. What do you think someone's *avocation* would be? (Hint: The *a* in *avocation* is from *ā, ab*, which means "away.")

Someone's avocation is what he or she does outside of, or "away" from, work. It is usually an activity or hobby that one does for enjoyment and pleasure.

A. New Vocabulary

Latin	English		
arō, arāre, arāvī, arātum	I plow, to plow, I plowed, plowed		
nāvigō, nāvigāre, nāvigāvī, nāvigātum	I sail, to sail, I sailed, sailed		
flō, flāre, flāvī, flātum	I blow, to blow, I blew, blown		
vocō, vocāre, vocāvī, vocātum	I call, to call, I called, called		
vītō, vītāre, vītāvī, vītātum	I avoid, to avoid, I avoided, avoided		
aurum, -ī	gold	colloquium, -ī	conversation
argentum, -ī	silver	cōnsilium, -ī	plan
bracchium, -ī	arm		

B. Review Vocabulary

Latin	English	Latin	English
antīquus, -a, -um	old	laetus, -a, -um	happy
serēnus, -a, -um	calm, bright, clear	miser, misera, miserum	miserable
īrātus, -a, -um	angry		

C. Chant   Give the imperfect-tense (past) verb endings and fill in the boxes.

	Singular	Plural
1st person	-bam	-bāmus
2nd person	-bās	-bātis
3rd person	-bat	-bant

D. Grammar   Fill in the blanks.

1. One Latin tense that is used to express things that happened in the past is the ___imperfect___ tense.

2. Tense is ___time___.

3. All verbs have ___person___, ___number___, and ___tense___.

Chapter Story

Along the Appian Way, Part 14

Marcus and Julia *ambulābant* (____walked____) around the *forum*
(__public square__) all morning. They hadn't found any *signum* (____sign____)
or information about the rider, but they did find out that this year's harvest was very *bonus*
(____good____), that the pottery was very fragile and not meant to be touched (or even
looked at too hard) by clumsy children, and that a Roman cohort was marching toward the
oppidum (____town____). Troop movements and patrols were fairly common, even
during peaceful times.

Now Marcus and Julia were chatting with an *agricola* (____farmer____) as he unloaded
corn from a cart next to his booth. "I don't remember seeing the messenger you describe, but
talk to my friend Priscus, the candlemaker." He pointed off to the distant booth at the *forum*
(__public square__). "He always seems to know about any important people passing through."

"Thanks!" Marcus and Julia both said.

"Want to race? I'll race you to that *monumentum* (____monument____)!" Julia shouted at
Marcus and then took off, not waiting for an answer.

Julia laughed as she dodged between the crowds, glancing back to be sure that Marcus
couldn't catch her. Marcus smiled as he played the *lūdus* (____game____) with Julia, but
he had noticed something that slowed him down.

In the darker corners of the *forum* (__public square__), a pair of eyes had begun to follow the
children and their movements. Marcus caught sight of a *vir* (____man____) who squinted
at Marcus before he turned away and crept deeper into the shadows. Marcus strained *vidēre*
(____to see____) him, but could not.

Marcus shivered and sprinted to catch up, still feeling a gaze on his back.

Grammar Lesson

Translating the Imperfect Tense

Remember how we said that there are several ways to show that something
happened in the past in English? Well, because of that, there are three different
possible ways to translate the imperfect tense. For example, were we to say,
"*Amābam*," there would be three possible translations:

"I loved" (rarely used)
"I was loving"
"I used to love"

Worksheet

A. Translation

1. **saxum** rock
2. **nauta** sailor
3. **vocās** you call
4. **ferrum** iron
5. **flābātis** you all were blowing
6. **Ars longa, vīta brevis.** Art is long, life is brief.

7. **agricolae** (nom.) farmers
8. **vidēbam** I was seeing
9. **monumentī** (gen.) of the monument
10. **valla** walls
11. **vēlō** (abl.) from the sail/curtain

B. Chant

Give the imperfect-tense verb endings and fill in the boxes.

	Singular	Plural
1st person	-bam	-bāmus
2nd person	-bās	-bātis
3rd person	-bat	-bant

C. Grammar

Parse each verb (person, number, tense), then give three possible translations for each and circle the recommended one.

1/P/I
1. **Amābāmus.** We loved.   ⊙We were loving.⊙   We used to love.

3/S/Pr
2. **Nāvigat.** ⊙He sails.⊙   He is sailing.   He does sail.

D. Derivatives

1. A ___verb___ is a type of word that shows action. (*verbum*)

2. A traffic ___signal/sign___ lets drivers know when they should stop or go. (*signum*)

Derivatives

A. Study

Study the English derivatives that come from the Latin words you have learned this week:

Latin	English
ferrum	ferric, ferrous
folium	foliate, exfoliate, foliage, foil, folio
monumentum	monument, monumental
pābulum	pabulum, pablum
saxum	saxicolous **TN**
signum	signal, sign, significant, resign, resignation, assign
silentium	silent, silence
vāllum	wall
vēlum	veil, veiled, reveal, revelation
verbum	verb, verbiage, verbal, verbally, verbalize, verbose, verbosity, verbatim, proverb, proverbial

Fun Fact!

Generally, ancient Romans had naturally healthy teeth and gums, thanks to their low-sugar diet. But their teeth did wear out because of their gritty flour. They were known to make false teeth from bone or ivory.

B. Define

Teacher's Note: Students often think that the words "saxophone" and "Saxon" are Latin derivatives, but they actually come from the Old English *Seaxe*.

In a dictionary, look up two of the English derivatives from the list above and write their definitions in the spaces below:

1. _____

2. _____

C. Apply

We derive quite a few words from the Latin word *verbum*. As you could probably guess, we get our word "verb" from *verbum*. A *verb* is a type of English word that shows action.

A *proverb* is a short saying or adage that contains a common truth and/or practical advice. The word "proverb" comes from the Latin *prō* (before, forth, on behalf of) and *verbum*. It means a group of words "put forth," meaning that a proverb is a group of common, well-known words that are put forth so that almost everyone has heard them. The Latin word for *proverb* is *prōverbium*. That's not very different from the English, is it?

The following are some *proverbs* you may have heard:

"Waste not, want not."
"A friend in need is a friend indeed."
"Pride comes before a fall."

Write down two other *proverbs* that you have heard:

Answers will vary. Some examples include: Measure twice, cut once. Live by the **sword, die by the sword.**

A. New Vocabulary

Latin	English
ferrum, -ī	iron
folium, -ī	leaf
monumentum, -ī	monument
pābulum, -ī	food for animals (fodder)
saxum, -ī	rock
signum, -ī	sign
silentium, -ī	silence
vāllum, -ī	wall, rampart
vēlum, -ī	sail, curtain
verbum, -ī	word

B. Review Vocabulary

Latin	English
videō, vidēre, vīdī, vīsum	I see, to see, I saw, seen
teneō, tenēre, tenuī, tentum	I hold, to hold, I held, held
habeō, habēre, habuī, habitum	I have, to have, I had, had
iubeō, iubēre, iussī, iussum	I order, to order, I ordered, ordered
augeō, augēre, auxī, auctum	I increase, to increase, I increased, increased

Quiz

C. Chant Give the imperfect-tense chant and fill in the boxes.

	Singular	Plural
1st person	-bam	-bāmus
2nd person	-bās	-bātis
3rd person	-bat	-bant

D. Grammar Parse each verb, then give three translations of each and underline the recommended one.

2/P/I
1. **Arābātis.** You (all) plowed.   <u>You (all) were plowing.</u>   You (all) used to plow.

3/S/Pr
2. **Vītat.** <u>He avoids.</u>   He is avoiding.   He does avoid.

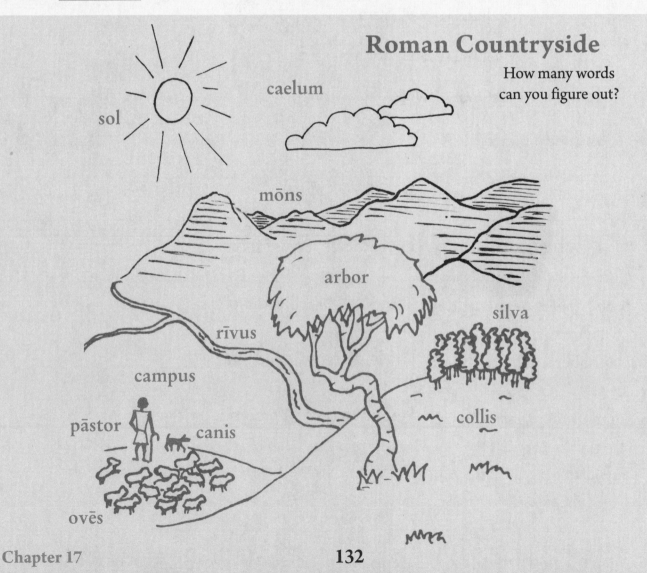

Roman Countryside

How many words can you figure out?

caelum

sol

mōns

arbor

silva

rīvus

campus

pāstor   canis

collis

ovēs

Chapter 18

Let's review our Latin words from the last four chapters. Check the ones you have not mastered, and then spend extra time chanting those words until you have mastered them. For additional practice, write out the English translations for each Latin word.

VERBS

Chapter 14	Chapter 16
❑ videō <u>I see</u>	❑ arō <u>I plow</u>
❑ teneō <u>I hold</u>	❑ nāvigō <u>I sail</u>
❑ habeō <u>I have</u>	❑ flō <u>I blow</u>
❑ iubeō <u>I order</u>	❑ vocō <u>I call</u>
❑ augeō <u>I increase</u>	❑ vītō <u>I avoid</u>

NOUNS

Chapter 14	Chapter 16
❑ agricola, -ae <u>farmer</u>	❑ aurum, -ī <u>gold</u>
❑ nauta, -ae <u>sailor</u>	❑ argentum, -ī <u>silver</u>
❑ poēta, -ae <u>poet</u>	❑ bracchium, -ī <u>arm</u>
❑ incola, -ae <u>settler</u>	❑ colloquium, -ī <u>conversation</u>
❑ ager, agrī <u>field</u>	❑ cōnsilium, -ī <u>plan</u>

Chapter 15	Chapter 17
❑ animus, -ī <u>mind</u>	❑ ferrum, -ī <u>iron</u>
❑ campus, -ī <u>level space, plain, field</u>	❑ folium, -ī <u>leaf</u>
❑ annus, -ī <u>year</u>	❑ monumentum, -ī <u>monument</u>
❑ mūrus, -ī <u>wall</u>	❑ pābulum, -ī <u>food for animals (fodder)</u>
❑ cibus, -ī <u>food</u>	❑ saxum, -ī <u>rock</u>
❑ ventus, -ī <u>wind</u>	❑ signum, -ī <u>sign</u>
❑ equus, -ī <u>horse</u>	❑ silentium, -ī <u>silence</u>
❑ ferus, -ī <u>wild animal</u>	❑ vāllum, -ī <u>wall, rampart</u>
❑ fluvius, -ī <u>river</u>	❑ vēlum, -ī <u>sail, curtain</u>
	❑ verbum, -ī <u>word</u>

Derivative Study

Here are some more derivatives that come from Latin root words. Choose three favorites from each column and circle them.

Verbs:

videō. . . . . video (movie), vision, visionary, evident

teneō. . . . . tenacious, tenure, tenet, tenacity, tenant

habeō . . . . habit, habitual, habituate

iubeō. . . . . jussive

augeō . . . . augment, augmentation

Nouns:

ager . . . . agriculture, agricultural

poēta. . . . . poet, poetry, poetic

agricola . . . . agriculture, agricultural

nauta. . . . . nautical (relating to seamen, ships, or navigation)

animus . . . . animate, animated (spirited, moving), animator, animation, inanimate

campus. . . . . camp, campus

annus . . . . annual

mūrus . . . . mural

ventus. . . . . vent

equus . . . . equestrian

ferus . . . . feral (wild), ferocious

fluvius. . . . . fluvial (relating to a stream or river)

Verbs:

arō . . . . arable (fit for farming)

nāvigō. . . . . navigate, navigation, navigator, circumnavigate

flō. . . . . inflate, inflation, flatulence

vocō. . . . . vocal, vocation, vocalize, invoke, evoke, provoke, revoke

vītō. . . . . inevitable (don't confuse with *vīta, -ae,* life)

Nouns:

aurum. . . . . auric (of or relating to gold)

argentum. . . . . Argentina (land of silver)

bracchium. . . . . . . brace, embrace, bracelet

colloquium. . . . . . colloquial

cōnsilium . . . . counsel

ferrum . . . . ferric (of or relating to iron), ferrous

folium. . . . . foliate, exfoliate, foliage, foil

monumentum . . . . monument, monumental

pābulum . . . . pabulum, pablum

saxum. . . . . saxicolous **TN**

signum . . . . signal, sign, significant, resign, assign

silentium. . . . . silent, silence

vāllum. . . . . wall

vēlum . . . . veil, veiled, reveal, revelation

verbum. . . . . verb, verbal, verbose (using a lot of words), verbosity, verbalize, verbatim, proverb, proverbial

> **Teacher's Note:** As noted in chapter 17, "Saxon" comes from the Old English *Seaxe.*

As you have done before, choose one English derivative from each column (above) and try to find them in a good dictionary that has Latin roots. Do you remember how to do this? Review chapter 5 ("Working with Derivatives" section) if you need a reminder. In the spaces below, list the derivatives you looked up and their Latin roots. The first one is filled out for you.

1. English Derivative: *ferocious*　　　　　　Latin Root: *ferus, -a, -um* (wild)

2. English Derivative: _____　　Latin Root: _____

3. English Derivative: _____　　Latin Root: _____

SN V **The girl walks.**	SN V **The sailor holds.**
SN V **Puella ambulat.**	SN V **Nauta tenet.**
SN LV PrN **The girl is a student.**	SN V **Incola pugnat.**
SN LV PrN **Puella est discipula.**	SN V **Poēta dēmōnstrat.**
SN LV PrN **Puer est discipulus.**	SN LV PrN **Poēta est fēmina.**
SN V **Vir videt.**	SN LV PrN **Fēmina est poēta.**
SN V **Fēmina iubet.**	SN LV PrN **Vir est aquārius.**
SN V **The woman orders.**	SN LV PrN **Puer est amīcus.**

Tense is Time

The word "tense" comes from the Latin word *tempus*, which means "time" (an event is *temporary* when it lasts a short time). When we talk about a verb's tense, we are talking about the "time" in which a verb's action takes place. If a verb takes place in the present, it is called the *present* tense! If it takes place in the past, it may be called a *past* tense. However, in Latin there are different ways to show that something happened in the past. One way is to use a past tense called the *imperfect* tense.

Do you remember the three ways of translating the **present** tense?
There are three ways to translate *amō*: "I love," "I am loving," "I do love."

Do you remember the three ways of translating the **imperfect** tense?
There are three ways to translate *amābam*: "I loved," "I was loving," "I used to love." Give the three ways of translating the following verbs that are in the imperfect tense.

vidēbam: I saw   ,   I was seeing ,   I used to see

tenēbās: you held   , you were holding , you used to hold

nāvigābat: he sailed ,   he was sailing ,   he used to sail

flābāmus: we blew   ,   we were blowing ,   we used to blow

vocābātis: you all called , you all were calling , you all used to call

habēbant: they had ,   they were having ,   they used to have

Along the Appian Way, Part 15

While Julia happily showed the candlemaker the seal on Marcus's scroll, she didn't notice that Marcus had circled back around, closer to the *locus* (____place____) where the strange man was. He wanted *spectāre* (____to look at____) him more closely—to get a chance to see who it was that he had seen watching them so carefully. Marcus crept along, keeping close to a *mūrus* (____wall____) in the shadows. He ducked behind a soup seller and scrambled under the *mēnsa* (____table____) of the toga seller.

Marcus was able *iacēre/jacēre* (____to lie down____) under the table, then he peered out from between the folds of cloth and saw a shadowy *vir* (____man____) watching Julia intently. The *vir* (____man____) glanced around and shrugged, muttering something to himself. The *vir* (____man____) was likely wondering where Marcus went. He wasn't sure what the man was up to, but he was quite certain that he didn't want the man to find him. He wanted to turn and run, but felt he had to find out more about the suspicious *vir* (____man____). The *vir* (____man____) had unusual markings on his hands and *bracchia* (____arms____)—strange tattoos. Marcus had to get a closer in order *vidēre* (____to see____) him.

Marcus carefully moved closer, first ducking behind a small group of ladies haggling over the price of one of the togas, and then quickly following a large *vir* (____man____) carrying a *magnus* (____large____) basket before silently crouching behind a *mēnsa* (____table____) topped with several round, pale cabbages. As Marcus leaned around the *mēnsa* (____table____) leg, he saw the tattoo markings were of snakes crisscrossing the stranger's arms. The heads of the snakes led all the way up to the top of the man's hand. As the stranger stroked his chin, it was as if the snakes were moving back and forth, looking for something.

Marcus swallowed hard.

Grammar Lesson

Future Tense

In the last lesson we discussed one of the ways in which we can talk about things that happened in the past. That was the imperfect tense. Now we are going to discuss the future tense. We use the future tense when we talk about things that haven't happened yet. To put a verb in the future tense, all that you need to do is find the stem (you're familiar with that) and add the future endings to it. The endings for the future tense are listed in the weekly chant at the beginning of this chapter: *-bō, -bis, -bit, -bimus, -bitis, -bunt*!

Translating the Future Tense

Just like the imperfect tense, there are different ways of translating the future tense. Here are the options for translating the verb *amābō*:

I will love
I will be loving

You may be wondering why it is that there are so many ways to translate these different tenses. The answer is simple. In English we have fourteen different tenses, but there are only six different tenses in Latin! You didn't know there were so many different English tenses, did you? Don't worry, we're not going to talk about them all now. But, to satisfy your inexhaustible curiosity, here's a chart that matches up all of the Latin tenses that we've studied so far with the corresponding English tenses. The most important ones to remember for right now, though, are the ones that are in **bold**. It isn't important for you to memorize all these grammatical terms just yet, but it is important that you can translate Latin verbs from the first three tenses correctly.

	Example	English Translation (default translation in bold)	English Tense (default translation in bold)
1st person	**amō**	**I love**, I am loving, I do love	**Simple Present**, Present Progressive, Present Emphatic
2nd person	**amābam**	I loved, **I was loving**, I used to love **TN**	Simple Past, **Past Progressive**
3rd person	**amābō**	**I will love**, I will be loving	**Simple Future**, Future Progressive

Sculpture: Marble head of a Roman god, 1st or 2nd century AD

Teacher's Note: This is another version of the past progressive, as is "I kept on loving."

Worshet

A. Translation

1. **folium** <u>leaf</u>

2. **exerceō** <u>I train</u>

3. **cōgitō** <u>I think</u>

4. **doleō** <u>I suffer</u>

5. **mūtō** <u>I change</u>

6. **Scrībere est agere.** <u>To write is to act.</u>

7. **iaceō** <u>I lie down</u>

8. **caveō** <u>I guard against</u>

9. **capillus** <u>hair</u>

10. **humus** <u>ground, earth, land</u>

11. **inimīcus** <u>enemy (personal)</u>

B. Chant

Give the future-tense verb endings and fill in the boxes.

	Singular	**Plural**
1st person	-bō	-bimus
2nd person	-bis	-bitis
3rd person	-bit	-bunt

C. Grammar

1. The <u>future</u> tense is used to express things that have not yet happened.

2. Parse and translate the following verbs:

    1/S/F
a. **exercēbō** <u>I will train</u>

    3/S/I
b. **dolēbat** <u>he was suffering</u>

    3/S/Pr
c. **cavet** <u>he guards against</u>

    1/P/F
d. **iacēbimus** <u>we will lie down</u>

D. Derivatives

1. To be healthy, everyone should engage in physical <u>exercise</u>. (*exerceō*)

2. A <u>capillary</u> is a hairlike blood vessel. (*capillus*)

Derivatives

A. Study

Study the English derivatives that come from the Latin words you have learned this week:

Latin	English
caveō	caveat
doleō	doleful, dolorous, indolent
exerceō	exercise
gaudeō	gaudy
iaceō/jaceō	adjacent
deus	deity, deify
capillus	capillary
humus	humble, humility, humus
inimīcus	inimical, enmity
locus	location, local, locale, dislocation, relocation

Fun Fact!

Roman roads were primarily built by soldiers. These roads were critical to moving troops quickly around the empire, and were built so well that they lasted for centuries.
What modern structures do you think will last that long?

B. Define

In a dictionary, look up two of the English derivatives from the list above and write their definitions in the spaces below:

1. _____

2. _____

C. Apply

The first derivative listed this week is the word "caveat." This word is a true Latin word, imported directly into English. When this happens, we call it a "loan word." In Latin, *caveat* means "let him beware, or let him guard against." There is a famous phrase from Latin that has come into English: *Caveat emptor*, which means "let the buyer beware" (*emptor* means "buyer"). What this phrase means is that when you are shopping, you should be careful to make sure that you are not being cheated and paying good money for a bad product. In English, the word "caveat" has come to mean a warning. **Example:** "His father let him go to the carnival with one *caveat*—he must not ride the old Ferris wheel."

If you were a farmer, you would know what *humus* is. *Humus* is another loan word that has been imported directly from Latin into English. In English, *humus* is dark, rich, fertile soil that is full of nutrients. Farmers and gardeners really like *humus*! Note that we also get the words *humble* and *humility* from the Latin word *humus*. To be *humble* is to be "near to the earth" rather than proud and "raised up high."

Write two sentences using different derivatives from the word *humus*:

1. <u>Example: Though she was a famous pianist, she was known for her humility.</u>

2. <u>Example: He was a little-known man from a humble town.</u>

A. New Vocabulary

Latin	English
caveō, cavēre, cāvī, cautum	I guard against, to guard against, I guarded against, guarded against
doleō, dolēre, doluī, dolitum	I suffer, to suffer, I suffered, suffered
exerceō, exercēre, exercuī, exercitum	I train, to train, I trained, trained
gaudeō, gaudēre, gavīsus sum	I rejoice, to rejoice, I rejoiced
iaceō, iacēre, iacuī	I lie down, to lie down, I lay down
deus, -ī	god
capillus, -ī	hair
humus, -ī	earth, ground, land
inimīcus, -ī	enemy (personal)
locus, -ī	place

B. Review Vocabulary

Latin	English
monumentum, ī	monument
ventus, -ī	wind
dubitō, dubitāre, dubitāvī, dubitātum	I doubt, to doubt, I doubted, doubted
fātum, -ī	fate
forum, -ī	public square

Quiz

C. Chant Give the future-tense chant and fill in the boxes.

	Singular	Plural
1st person	-bō	-bimus
2nd person	-bis	-bitis
3rd person	-bit	-bunt

D. Grammar Give the definition or answer the question for each item below.

1. When do you use the future-tense endings?

   When something hasn't happened yet.

2. Translate the following verbs:

   a. **amābō** I will love

   b. **exercet** he trains

   c. **dubitābat** he was doubting

Latin Today: Military Ranks

- **Private:** from *privātus* (not in public life, withdrawn).
- **Corporal:** originally from the Italian *capo caporale* (head of a body, as in a body of soldiers). *Capo* is from the Latin *caput* (head).
- **Sergeant:** from the French *sergent*, which came from the Latin *serviēns* (serving).
- **Lieutenant:** from the French *lieu* (place) and *tenant* (holding). *Tenant* is from the Latin *tenēns* (holding). A lieutenant could hold the place of a superior officer if need be, just like a lieutenant governor can stand in the place of a governor.
- **Captain:** from the late Latin *capitāneus* (chief), which is related to the Latin word *caput* (head).
- **Major:** from the Latin *maior* or *major* (greater).
- **Colonel:** from the Italian *colonello*, which came from the Latin *columna* (column), so named because such an officer originally led the first column of a regiment of soldiers.
- **General:** from *generālis* (relating to all). A *general* is an officer in charge of all of an army.

Along the Appian Way, Part 16

"Thank you, sir." Julia said to the candlemaker as Marcus slid up beside her. "Where have you been?" she asked Marcus.

Marcus leaned in, "I want to tell you something, but I don't want you *clamāre* (_____to shout_____), OK?"

Julia sighed and nodded, "Uh-huh."

Marcus whispered even quieter, "We're being watched."

"WHO'S WATCHING US?!" Julia's head shot up and she quickly began scanning in every direction. Marcus yanked on her *brachium* (_____arm_____), and pulled her down to crouch beside him.

"I told you not *clamāre* (_____to shout_____)!" Marcus grumbled as he glanced around. "Oh, right."

"We need to *ambulāre* (_____to walk_____). Let's walk over to that *casa* (_____house_____) and try get under the *tectum* (_____roof_____)." Marcus towed Julia after him, both of them hunched over, trying to hide behind other shoppers.

"Who would want *spectāre* (_____to look at_____) us? Is it someone we know? What do they want? What's their *cōnsilium* (_____plan_____)?"

Marcus looked around and then led Julia into a skinny alley. "Look," he turned and finally gave her his attention, "I don't know, but *cōgitō* (_____I think_____) they're interested in the scroll."

"But why?"

"Are you even listening to me? How should I know?!"

"Do we need *vitāre* (_____to avoid_____) them? Where are they now?"

Marcus peeked back to where the *vīr* (_____man_____) had been. He was gone.

"Excuse me, children," a voice said out of nowhere.

Marcus and Julia spun around. The first thing Marcus saw was a *bracchium* (_____arm_____) with a snake tattoo.

Grammar Lesson

The Accusative Case Part I: Direct Objects

A linking verb is like an = sign in math.

So far, all of our nouns (and adjectives) have been in the **nominative** case. Now we're going to talk about the next Latin case, the **accusative** case. Remember that, in Latin, the case tells you the noun job, the role that the noun has in the sentence. While the most common use of the **nominative** case is for the **subject** of the sentence (the noun that the sentence is all about), the most common use of the **accusative** case is for the **direct object**. Have you learned what a direct object is in your English grammar class yet? In case you haven't, **the direct object receives the action of the verb**. For example, if someone were to say, "I love Latin," "Latin" would be the direct object. "I" is the subject; it tells you who is doing the action. "Love" is the verb; it tells you what is being done. "Latin," however, is the thing that is being loved.

Now, if a direct object receives the action of a verb, it stands to reason that the verb has to be an action verb. Do you remember the difference between an action verb and a linking verb? **An action verb tells what the subject does, whereas a linking verb tells you what the subject is.** In order for the subject to be doing something *to* someone or something else, it must be doing something in the first place. Therefore, in order to have a direct object, you must first have an action verb. In fact, it has to be a special kind of action verb called a **transitive** verb. Thus, a transitive verb is defined as **a type of action verb that takes an object**. We label a direct object with *DO* and a transitive verb with *V-T*.

TN

As we mentioned, in Latin, a direct object is in the accusative case. Thus, in the example above, we would translate the sentence "I love the family" as *Amō familiam*. We would label it:

V-T DO
Amō familiam.

Here are a few other examples. Can you tell which word is the direct object? Look at the ending, not the word order.*

SN DO V-T
Vir lupum oppugnat.

SN V-T DO
Puerī explōrant silvam.

SN V-T DO
Dominus cavet pātriam.

Teacher's Note: It may be helpful to note to students that one way to remember transitive verbs is to think of the word "*transi-tive*" as sharing a root with the word "*trans*fer": a transitive verb *transfers* its action to an object. Students will learn the preposition *trans* (which means "across") in chapter 25.

*Note that when using direct objects in Latin, we can vary the placement or word order, even placing the object of the verb before the verb!

Worksheet

A. Translation

1. casa __house__
2. epistulam __letter (acc.)__
3. fāmās __rumors, reports, fame__
4. sepulchrum __tomb__
5. augēbis __You will increase__
6. Scrībere est agere. __To write is to act.__

7. capitula __chapters, headings__
8. laetus __happy__
9. tēctum __roof__
10. nāvigābant __They were sailing__
11. deās __goddesses (acc.)__

B. Chant
Give the nominative- and accusative-case noun endings that you have learned.

	First Declension		Second Declension		Second Declension (N)	
	S	P	S	P	S	P
Nominative	-a	-ae	-us	-ī	-um	-a
Accusative	-am	-ās	-um	-ōs	-um	-a

C. Grammar

1. A ___transitive___ verb is an action verb that takes an object.

2. All ___direct___ objects are in the ___accusative___ case.

3. Label and translate the following sentences.

      SN   DO   V-T
  a. Lupus virum necat. __The wolf kills the man.__

      DO   SN   V-T
  b. Agrōs puellae explōrant. __The girls explore the fields.__

      SN   V-T   DO
  c. Ventus flat vēlum. __The wind blows the sail/curtain.__

D. Derivatives

1. "___Sepulchre___" is a fancy word for tomb. (sepulchrum)

2. The ___epistles___ of Paul were letters written to various churches and individual Christians. (epistula)

Derivatives

A. Study

Study the English derivatives that come from the Latin words you have learned this week:

Latin	English
dea	deity, deify
casa	casa (Spanish for "house")
epistula	epistle, epistolary
fāma	fame, famous, famed, infamy, infamous
familia	family, familiar, familiarize, familiarity
beneficium	benefit, beneficial, beneficiary
sepulchrum	sepulchre
capitulum	chapter, capitol, capital
tēctum	tectonics
templum	temple, template, contemplate, contemplative

Fun Fact!

Roman emperors would build large bathhouses to show off their wealth and power. These baths could contain several large pools of differing temperatures and other features for leisure activity, such as libraries. *But don't take your books into the pool!*

B. Define

In a dictionary, look up two of the English derivatives from the list above and write their definitions in the spaces below:

1. _____

2. _____

C. Apply

The word *capitulum* is related to another Latin word, *caput*, which means "head." A *capitulum* can be defined as a "little head." The little head or heading at the beginning of a new section in a book introduces a new chapter. Therefore, *capitulum* can mean "chapter," too. There are quite a few other words that are derived from *capitulum*, including "capitol" and "capital." A *capitol* building is usually built at the highest point in a city and certainly is the building that contains the leaders, or "heads," of the government. In fact, in ancient Rome, the chief temple to Zeus was built on a high hill called Capitoline Hill. If something is of *capital* importance, it is very important, at the "head" of the list. *Capital* punishment is the "highest" form of punishment someone can receive—death.

Can you think of a type of hat whose name is taken from the Latin word *caput*?

Cap _____

A. New Vocabulary

Latin	English
dea, -ae	goddess
casa, -ae	house
epistula, -ae	letter
fāma, -ae	rumor, report, fame
familia, -ae	family
beneficium, -ī	benefit, gift
sepulchrum	tomb
capitulum, -ī	heading, chapter
tēctum, -ī	roof
templum, -ī	temple

B. Review Vocabulary

Latin	English
flō, flāre, flāvī, flātum	I blow, to blow, I blew, blown
habeō, habēre, habuī, habitum	I have, to have, I had, had
serēnus, -a, -um	calm, bright, clear
mandō, mandāre, mandāvī, mandātum	I entrust, to entrust, I entrusted, entrusted

Quiz

C. Chant   Give the nominative- and accusative-case noun endings that you have learned.

	First Declension		Second Declension		Second Declension (N)	
	S	**P**	**S**	**P**	**S**	**P**
Nominative	-a	-ae	-us	-ī	-um	-a
Accusative	-am	-ās	-um	-ōs	-um	-a

D. Grammar   Give the definition or answer the question for each item below.

1. Transitive verb:

   An action verb that takes an object.

2. Direct object:

   The noun that receives the action of the verb.

3. What noun job is always in the accusative case?

   direct object

Drawing: *The Porta Maggiore in Rome* by Daniël Dupré, 1789

Chapter Story

Along the Appian Way, Part 17

The *vir* (_____man_____) with the tattoo smiled as he lowered himself to the level of the children. "Hello, *cārī* (_____dear_____) children. I couldn't help but notice that you had a scroll there. Oh, and look at that seal of *aurum* (_____gold_____). Are you *parātus* (_____ready_____) to sell it?"

He wore a blue tunic and had short, curly, black *capillus* (_____hair_____). His smile was friendly and he didn't look nearly as scary as he had standing in the shadows.

Marcus and Julia *spectābant* (_____looked at_____) each other and tried not to look nervous. What was the right answer?! A long *silentium* (_____silence_____) hung in the air.

"Um . . ." Marcus cleared his throat. "I suppose that would depend on how much someone might want to pay for it."

The *vir* (_____man_____) looked down and reached for the pouch on his belt.

Julia opened her mouth wide to gasp. She couldn't believe that Marcus would really sell the scroll, but Marcus squeezed her hand as a *signum* (_____sign_____) and took a step back. Julia followed.

"It's a pretty valuable scroll, *cēnseō* (_____I estimate_____), but *dābimus* (_____we will give_____) it to you for the right price—a few bits of *argentum* (_____silver_____). Right, Julia?"

The man glanced back up with one hand still on his belt.

"I . . . I would have to agree," Julia said, trying to put on her best smile. "Especially if you didn't act like a criminal."

Marcus gasped.

The *vir* (_____man_____) scowled and lunged for the scroll.

The two kids jumped back and ran down the alley!

Grammar Lesson

Eram, erās, erat . . . The Imperfect of *Sum*

The verb *sum, esse* has tenses, too. Remember that tense is time. The tense tells us when something happens. If we mean that something is a certain way now, we use the present tense. Just as with other verbs, we could use the imperfect tense if we wanted to say that something was a certain way in the past.

Worksheet

A. Translation

1. **monēbimus** we will warn
2. **clārus** clear, famous
3. **audēbant** they were daring
4. **parātus** prepared
5. **manēs** you remain
6. **Dictum, factum.** Said and done.
7. **lūgeō** I grieve
8. **dignus** worthy
9. **cavent** they guard against
10. **silva** forest
11. **campus** level space, plain, field

B. Chant
Give the imperfect-tense forms of *sum, esse.*

	Singular	Plural
1st person	eram: I was	erāmus: we were
2nd person	erās: you were	erātis: you all were
3rd person	erat: he was	erant: they were

C. Grammar
1. Direct object: The noun in the accusative case that receives the action of a transitive verb.
2. Transitive verb: An action verb that takes an object.

D. Parse, Label, and Translate

SN DO V-T
1. **Vir filium monet.** The man warns the son.
Nom/S/M Acc/S/M 3/S/Pr

SN LV PrA
2. **Dominus erat dignus.** The master was worthy.
Nom/S/M 3/S/I Nom/S/M

E. Derivatives

1. Every ten years the government conducts a **census** of all the people. (*cēnseō*)
2. The king walked into the court in a stately and **dignified** manner. (*dignus*)

A. New Vocabulary

Latin	English
audeō, audēre, ausus sum	I dare, to dare, I dared
lūgeō, lūgēre, lūxī, lūctum	I grieve, to grieve, I grieved, grieved
moneō, monēre, monuī, monitum	I warn, to warn, I warned, warned
maneō, manēre, mānsī, mānsum	I remain, to remain, I remained, remained
cēnseō, cēnsēre, cēnsuī, cēnsum	I estimate, to estimate, I estimated, estimated
parātus, -a, -um	prepared
cārus, -a, -um	dear
longus, -a, -um	long
dignus, -a, -um	worthy
clārus, -a, -um	clear, famous

B. Review Vocabulary

Latin	English
doleō, dolēre, doluī, dolitum	I suffer, to suffer, I suffered, suffered
pābulum, -ī	food for animals (fodder)

C. Chant   Give the imperfect-tense forms of *sum, esse* and fill in the boxes.

	Singular	Plural
1st person	eram: I was	erāmus: we were
2nd person	erās: you were	erātis: you all were
3rd person	erat: he was	erant: they were

D. Grammar   Provide definitions.

1. Direct object:

The noun in the accusative case that receives the action of a transitive verb.

2. Transitive verb:

An action verb that takes an object.

E. Parse, Label, and Translate

    SN   DO   V-T
1. **Agricola equum exercet.**   The farmer trains the horse.
Nom/S/M* Acc/S/M 3/S/Pr

    SN   LV PrA
2. **Magister est īrātus.**   The teacher is angry.
Nom/S/M 3/S/Pr Nom/S/M

*Agricola is one of the four masculine nouns of the first declension. See chapter 14.

Along the Appian Way, Part 18

Marcus and Julia burst out of the alley into the *lāta via* (broad road). They heard heavy footsteps trailing them closely.

Then, two more tattooed and *sordidī virī* (dirty men) suddenly appeared close by and joined the chase.

Young and *parvī* (small), the two children were able to weave and dodge between sellers and their carts as the *magnus vir* (large man) stumbled and shoved his way behind them.

Marcus jumped over small burlap bags stuffed with colorful spices. Julia slid under a *mēnsa* (table) filled with dates and raisins, just avoiding a grasping *bracchium* (arm). The tattooed man cursed as he slammed his shoulder against the *mēnsa* (table). Julia leaned against a nearby *mūrus* (wall) for a moment, breathing heavily, trying to be *tacitus* (silent) and *vītāre perīculum* (to avoid danger).

"Julia! Up here!" Marcus *vocābat* (called) from nearby.

Julia glanced around to see Marcus waving from a nearby scaffold. Julia quickly climbed up the scaffold that led onto the *tectum* (roof) as her pursuer came rushing forward. Just as Julia made it up, she pushed the boards off the *tectum* (roof). They crashed below, jolting and surprising the tattooed *vir* (man).

Leaping from *tectum* (roof) to *tectum* (roof), Marcus and Julia quickly put distance between them and their pursuers.

Grammar Lesson

The Accusative Case Part II: Objects of the Preposition

TN **A preposition is a little word that connects a noun or a pronoun to the rest of the sentence.** An example of a preposition in English is "to," as in the phrase "to the forest." That phrase can be attached to a sentence like this: "The man walks to the forest." The noun that the preposition connects to the rest of the sentence is called the **object of the preposition**. When you put together the preposition, its object, and all of the adjectives and articles and other

> **Teacher's Note:** Prepositions are "little" in Latin—almost always two short syllables or less.

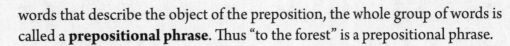
words that describe the object of the preposition, the whole group of words is called a **prepositional phrase**. Thus "to the forest" is a prepositional phrase.

In Latin, the word for "to" (in the sense of "to/toward") is *ad*. Thus, if we wanted to say "to the forest," it would be *ad silvam*. If we wanted to say "The man walks to the forest," it would be *Vir ad silvam ambulat*.

Did you notice what case the object of that preposition is in? If you didn't, look again. It's in the accusative case. In Latin, some prepositions are said to "take the accusative." That's just a way of saying that some prepositions will always have objects that are in the accusative case. Because some prepositions take a different case (the ablative case), it's important to remember which ones take which case. We're going to concentrate for a while on the accusative-case prepositions, starting with *ad*.

Let's take that sentence again and label all of its parts, putting parentheses around the prepositional phrase. Remember that we use *SN* for the subject noun and *V* for the verb. Let's use *PR* for preposition and *OP* for the object of the preposition. Labeling the sentence should look like this:

SN PR OP   V
Vir (ad silvam) ambulat.

Now try labeling a few on your own, and then translate each sentence.

SN PR OP V
Puer (ad silvam) errat.
The boy wanders to the forest.

SN PR OP   V
Nauta (ad insulam) nāvigat.
The sailor sails to the island.

SN   PR OP   V
Lupus (ad aquam) ambulat.
The wolf walks to the water.

Coin Mold: *Terra-cotta coin mold*, ca. AD 308–320

A. Translation

1. grātus _grateful_

2. dēfessus _tired_

3. tēctum _roof_

4. tacitus _silent_

5. arō _I plow_

6. Dictum, factum. _Said and done._

7. caecus _blind_

8. videō _I see_

9. ignāvus _cowardly_

10. mīrus _strange, wonderful_

11. horrendus _horrendous_

B. Chant   Give the present- and imperfect-tense forms of *sum*.

	Present		Imperfect	
	Singular	**Plural**	**Singular**	**Plural**
1st person	sum	sumus	eram	erāmus
2nd person	es	estis	erās	erātis
3rd person	est	sunt	erat	errant

C. Grammar   Provide definitions.

1. ___Prepositions___ are important little words that connect a noun or pronoun to the rest of the sentence.

2. The ___object___ of the ___preposition___ is the noun that the preposition connects to the rest of the sentence.

3. A ___prepositional___ ___phrase___ includes a preposition, an object of the preposition, and all the adjectives that are connected to the object of the preposition.

D. Derivatives

1. ___Miracles___ are strange and wonderful happenings. (*mīrus*)

2. A judge is responsible for ensuring ___justice___ in a court case. (*iūstus*)

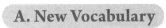

A. New Vocabulary

Latin	English
dēfessus, -a, -um	tired
sordidus, -a, -um	dirty
tacitus, -a, -um	silent
caecus, -a, -um	blind
grātus, -a, -um	grateful
ignāvus, -a, -um	cowardly
iūstus, -a, -um	just, fair, right
lātus, -a, -um	broad
mīrus, -a, -um	strange, wonderful
horrendus, -a, -um	horrendous

B. Review Vocabulary

Latin	English
capitulum, -ī	chapter, heading
vocō, vocāre, vocāvī, vocātum	I call, to call, I called, called
augeō, augēre, auxī, auctum	I increase, to increase, I increased, increased
malus, -a, -um	bad

C. Chant   Give the present- and imperfect-tense forms of *sum* and fill in the boxes.

	Present		Imperfect	
	Singular	Plural	Singular	Plural
1st person	sum	sumus	eram	erāmus
2nd person	es	estis	erās	erātis
3rd person	est	sunt	erat	errant

D. Grammar   On the lines provided, write the definition for each of the following items.

1. Preposition:

   A part of speech (or type of word) that connects a noun or a pronoun to the

   rest of the sentence.

2. Object of the preposition:

   The noun or pronoun that the preposition connects to the rest of the sentence.

3. Prepositional phrase:

   The group of words held together by the preposition and its object. It includes
   the preposition, the object of the preposition, and any adjectives that modify
   that object.

Chapter 23

Another four weeks of study and you have learned another forty words. As you did during the last review week, make sure you have these words mastered. Check the boxes of each word you don't know. Then review those words as much as you need to in order to master them. Remember to look at the words while chanting them.

Chapter 19	Chapter 21
❏ caveō __I guard against__	❏ audeō __I dare__
❏ doleō __I suffer__	❏ lūgeō __I grieve__
❏ exerceō __I train__	❏ moneō __I warn__
❏ gaudeō __I rejoice__	❏ maneō __I remain__
❏ iaceō __I lie down__	❏ cēnseō __I estimate__
❏ deus __god__	❏ parātus, -a, -um __prepared__
❏ capillus __hair__	❏ cārus, -a, -um __dear__
❏ humus __earth, ground, land__	❏ longus, -a, -um __long__
❏ inimīcus __enemy__	❏ dignus, -a, -um __worthy__
❏ locus __place__	❏ clārus, -a, -um __clear, famous__

Chapter 20	Chapter 22
❏ dea __goddess__	❏ dēfessus, -a, -um __tired__
❏ casa __house__	❏ sordidus, -a, -um __dirty__
❏ epistula __letter__	❏ tacitus, -a, -um __silent__
❏ fāma __rumor, report, fame__	❏ caecus, -a, -um __blind__
❏ familia __family__	❏ grātus, -a, -um __grateful__
❏ beneficium __benefit, gift__	❏ ignāvus, -a, -um __cowardly__
❏ sepulchrum __tomb__	❏ iūstus, -a, -um __just, fair, right__
❏ capitulum __heading, chapter__	❏ lātus, -a, -um __broad__
❏ tēctum __roof__	❏ mīrus, -a, -um __strange, wonderful__
❏ templum __temple__	❏ horrendus, -a, -um __horrendous__

List the words you still need to master here:

_____ _____ _____

_____ _____ _____

_____ _____ _____

Review

Grammar Review Future Tense for First and Second Conjugations (Ch. 19)

During the last unit, you learned the endings that we use to make the future tense. Do you have them mastered? Here they are:

	Singular	Plural
1st person	**-bō**	**-bimus**
2nd person	**-bis**	**-bitis**
3rd person	**-bit**	**-bunt**

Here is what they look like when connected to verbs from the first and second conjugations:

	Future 1st Conjugation		Future 2nd Conjugation	
	Singular	Plural	Singular	Plural
1st person	amā*bō*	amā*bimus*	vidē*bō*	vidē*bimus*
2nd person	amā*bis*	amā*bitis*	vidē*bis*	vidē*bitis*
3rd person	amā*bit*	amā*bunt*	vidē*bit*	vidē*bunt*

Note that verbs in the first conjugation have an *a* before the endings, as in *amābō*. Verbs in the second conjugation have an *e* before the endings, as in *vidēbō*. These vowels (before the endings) are called connecting vowels.

Translation Exercise Study the first box, then translate the sentences below.

Vir dolēbit.
The man will suffer.

Discipula errābit.
The student will wander.

Vir vigilābit.
The man will guard/keep watch.

Agricolae arābunt terram.
The farmers will plow the earth.

Magistra fābulam narrābit.
The teacher will tell a story.

Magister dēmōnstrābit epistulās.
The teacher will point out the letters.

Magistra fābulās narrābit.
The teacher will tell stories.

Fēminae gaudēbunt.

The women will rejoice.

Magistra discipulam vocābit.

The teacher will call the student.

Incolae explōrābunt terram.

The settlers will explore the earth.

Magistra discipulās exercēbit.

The teacher will train the students.

Magister dabit auxilium.

The teacher will give help.

Inimīcī oppidum oppugnābunt.

The enemies will attack the town.

Discipulī cōgitābunt.

The students will think.

Noun Jobs, Direct Objects, and the Accusative Case (Ch. 20)

You should remember that in Latin, nouns have cases: *nominative, genitive, dative, accusative,* and *ablative.* Do you remember the sentence we use to remember these cases?

Never Give Davus Any Apples. (N, G, D, A, A)

Remember that the subject in a sentence is the noun that is doing the action. The subject noun (SN) in Latin is always in the nominative case.

The direct object in a sentence is the noun that receives the action of the verb (labeled V-T). The direct object noun (labeled DO) is always in the accusative case.

SN	V-T	DO
Puella	**parat**	**epistulam.**
Nom.		Acc.

SN V-T DO
The girl prepares the letter.

In this sentence *puella* (girl) is in the nominative case because it is doing the action of preparing—*puella* is the subject of the sentence. *Epistulam* (letter) is in the accusative case because it is receiving the action of the verb—*epistulam* is the direct object in this sentence.

In the box below, label the Latin sentences and translate them into English.

SN V-T DO
Fēmina spectat famulam. The woman looks at the servant.

SN V-T DO
Vir exercet equum. The man trains the horse.

SN V-T DO
Puer cavet inimīcum. The boy guards against the enemy.

SN V-T DO
Puellae intrant casam. The girls enter the house.

In Latin, verbs often come at the end of a sentence, like these:

SN DO V-T
Pater fīlium monet. The father warns the son.

SN DO V-T
Fīlius sepulchrum spectat. The son looks at the tomb.

SN DO V-T
Fīliī lupum spectant. The sons look at the wolf.

SN DO V-T
Agricola humum arat. The farmer plows the ground.

Chapter 23

Grammar Review The Imperfect of *sum, esse*/Linking Verbs (Ch. 21)

	Present		Imperfect	
	Singular	Plural	Singular	Plural
1st person	**sum**: I am	**sumus**: we are	**eram**: I was	**erāmus**: we were
2nd person	**es**: you are	**estis**: you all are	**erās**: you were	**erātis**: you all were
3rd person	**est**: he/she/it is	**sunt**: they are	**erat**: he/she/it was	**erant**: they were

Do you remember your chants for the verb *sum, esse* (I am, to be)? The present tense is listed in the first box, above. The imperfect tense is listed in the second box. Can you chant them correctly with your eyes closed? Make sure you have these chants mastered.

When we use any of the forms of *sum, esse* in these chants, they will be used as linking verbs (LV), because they link a subject with another noun or adjective. Study these sentences:

SN LV PrN
Fēmina est poēta.
The woman is a poet.

A predicate nominative (PrN) is a noun that is "linked" with the subject noun.

SN LV PrA
Fēmina erat parva.
The woman was small.

A predicate adjective (PrA) is an adjective that is "linked" with the subject noun.

SN = Subject Noun
LV = Linking Verb
PrN = Predicate Nominative
PrA = Predicate Adjective

Study the sentences below and then translate and label the sentences that remain.

Linking Verbs with Nouns

SN   LV   PrN
Puella est poēta.   *The girl is a poet.*

SN   LV   PrN
Puellae sunt fīliae.   *The girls are daughters.*

SN   PrN   LV
Puer fīlius est.   *The boy is a son.* **TN**

SN   LV   PrN
Puerī erant discipulī.   The boys were students. _____

SN   PrN   LV
Puerī germānī sunt.   The boys are brothers. _____

SN   PrN   LV
Dominus amīcus erat.   The master was a friend. _____

Linking Verbs with Adjectives (Ch. 12)

SN   LV   PrA
Puella est laeta.   *The girl is happy.*

SN   LV   PrA
Puellae sunt īrātae.   *The girls are angry.*

SN   PrA   LV
Puer serēnus erat.   *The boy was calm.*

SN   LV   PrA
Puerī sunt miserī.   The boys are miserable. _____

SN   PrA   LV
Puerī bonī sunt.   The boys are good. _____

SN   PrA   LV
Dominus malus erat.   The master was bad. _____

Teacher's Note: Note the varied placement of the linking verbs in these sentences. Linking verbs such as *est*, *erat*, and *sum* can be placed in the middle or at the end of a Latin sentence.

Along the Appian Way, Part 19

Marcus hunched over next to an *aedificium* (_____building_____), trying to catch his breath. Julia scanned the passersby for any *signum* (_____sign_____) of the tattooed *vir* (_____man_____). A troop of Roman soldiers slowly marched by.

Julia lowered herself to the *humus* (_____ground_____) next to Marcus.

"Those snake men with the black *capilli* (_____hair_____) are our *inimīci* (_____enemies_____)!" whispered Julia. "Why?"

"I don't know." Marcus whispered.

"Look," said Marcus as he pointed at some nearby laundry. "If we borrow these togas set *extrā casam* (_____outside of the house_____) to dry, we could use them as disguises."

"And then *ambulābimus ad* (__we walk toward__) home?"

"Yes. It should help us to keep clear of those *mali et horrendi viri* (__bad and horrendous_____ men_____)."

"You have to admit," Julia said, "that was pretty fun, wasn't it?"

"Fun?! *Cōgitas* (_____You think_____) that was fun?! I never want to do that again in my whole life! I wish I had never gotten this scroll," Marcus growled as he waved the now-crumpled scroll in the air. "It has been nothing but—"

"I'll take it, then," a gruff voice said as a hand yanked the scroll away from Marcus.

Spinning around, Marcus and Julia were confronted by the snake man looming above them.

Grammar Lesson

Future Tense of *Sum*

At the beginning of the chapter is the future tense of *sum, esse*. When you want to express how things will be in the future, use these forms of the verb. Now we have three tenses for *sum, esse*. The present tense is used when we want to describe how things **are**; the imperfect tense is used when we want to explain how things **were**; and, finally, the future tense is used when we want to describe how things **will be**. Once again, here's that chant chart with the translations (including the proper personal pronouns) filled in so you can see how the forms are translated.

A. Translation

1. ad __to, toward__

2. ante __before__

3. sordidus __dirty__

4. apud __at, by, near__

5. circā __around__

6. **Docendō, discimus.** __By teaching, we learn.__

7. contrā __against__

8. infrā __below__

9. casa __house__

10. inter __between, among__

11. argentum __silver__

B. Chant   Give future tense of *sum*.

	Singular	**Plural**
1st person	erō: I will be	erimus: we will be
2nd person	eris: you will be	eritis: you all will be
3rd person	erit: he/she/it will be	erunt: they will be

C. Grammar   Parse and translate the following verbs.

1. **erimus** __we will be__
   1/P/F

2. **audēbās** __you were daring__
   2/S/I

3. **cēnsēmus** __we estimate__
   1/P/Pr

D. Derivatives

1. If *bellum* means "war," *antebellum* means __before the war__ .

2. Something that is outside of the ordinary can be called __extraordinary__ . (*extrā*)

Derivatives

A. Study

Study the English derivatives that come from the Latin words you have learned this week:

Latin	English
ad	add, address, adjective, administer, admit
ante	antebellum, antecedent, anteroom
circa	circus, circle, circulate, circumstance, circumnavigate
contrā	contrary, contradict, contrast, contraband
extrā	extraordinary, extraterrestrial, extracurricular, extrovert
infrā	infrared, infrastructure
inter	interest, intersperse, interact, intercede, intercept, interchange, interface, interfere, interfaith, interstate
intrā	introvert, intravenous
iuxtā/juxtā	juxtapose, juxtaposition

Fun Fact!

The most common Roman dinner was a porridge made from wheat. For fancy meals, the main course could feature as many as seven dishes. Possible dishes included oysters, eels, snails, duck, and peacock. Dessert was often honey cakes with fruit and nuts.

B. Define

In a dictionary, look up two of the English derivatives from the list above and write their definitions in the spaces below:

1. _____

2. _____

C. Apply

All of the words in the list above are prepositions. The word "preposition" comes from the compound Latin word *praepositiō*, which is made up of two words—*prae* ("before") and *positiō* ("setting, placing"). Would you be surprised to learn that all our "grammar" words come from Latin? Look up the following grammatical terms in your dictionary and write down both their definitions and the Latin root words from which they came.

	Definition	Latin Root
Verb	A word that expresses action or a state of being.	verbum (word)
Adverb	A word that modifies a verb.	ad + verbum (to the verb)
Noun	A word that is a person, place, thing, or state of being.	nōmen (name)
Pronoun	A word that takes the place of a noun.	prō + nōmen (for/in the place of the noun)
Adjective	A word that modifies a noun.	adjectīvus (attached)

A. New Vocabulary

Latin	English
ad	to, toward
ante	before
apud	at, by, near
circā	around
contrā	against
extrā	outside of
īnfrā	below
inter	between, among
intrā	within
iuxtā	near, next to

B. Review Vocabulary

Latin	English
dēfessus, -a, -um	tired
templum, -ī	temple
flō, flāre, flāvī, flātum	I blow, to blow, I blew, blown
teneō, tenēre, tenuī, tentum	I hold, to hold, I held, held
laetus, -a, -um	happy

C. Chant   Give the future tense of *sum* and fill in the labels.

	Singular	Plural
1st person	erō: I will be	erimus: we will be
2nd person	eris: you will be	eritis: you all will be
3rd person	erit: he/she/it will be	erunt: they will be

D. Grammar   Parse and translate the following verbs.

(3/P/I)
1. **erant** <u>they were</u>

(2/S/Pr)
2. **monēs** <u>you warn</u>

(1/P/I)
3. **manēbāmus** <u>we were remaining</u>

The Romance Languages

The Romance languages are those languages that evolved directly from the common, or Vulgar, Latin spoken by common people throughout the Roman Empire. The word "romantic," as in "romantic novels," emerged because in the Middle Ages tales of love and attraction were not written in the more formal classical Latin, but in the style of the Vulgar Latin, also called "Roman Latin."

The common Latin spoken everywhere in the Roman Empire blended with the native tongues of the lands the empire conquered, and evolved, gradually becoming several distinct but very much related languages. Six of the most common Romance languages today are Spanish, Portuguese, French, Italian, Romanian, and Catalan. By learning Latin, you are well on your way to learning any of these Romance languages.

The following are six of the Romance languages ranked by the number of people who speak them:

Language	No. of People	Countries
Spanish	400 million	Spain, Mexico, much of South America, Central America, Caribbean
Portuguese	200 million	Portugal, Brazil, six African countries, East Timor, Macau
French	100 million	France, Canada, Caribbean, some countries of Africa
Italian	62 million	Italy, immigrant communities in North and South America, Australia, and some African countries
Romanian	32 million	Romania, secondary language for many in Israel
Catalan	6.7 million	Spain, France, Andorra, Balearic Islands

Source: *Encyclopedia Britannica*, s.v. "Romance Languages."

Along the Appian Way, Part 20

The two other *virī* (_____men_____) grabbed Marcus and Julia from behind and *tenebant* (____they held____) them fast. Marcus tried *pugnāre* (____to fight____), but it was no use.

In front of them, the tattooed *vir* (_____man_____) held up the scroll in the afternoon light, carefully studying the *aurum* (_____gold_____) seal.

Marcus squirmed in his captor's grasp. "Let us g—" One of the *virī* (_____men_____) clamped a firm hand over Marcus's mouth.

"You should have done the right thing, *puer* (_____boy_____), and just given the scroll to me when I asked you kindly," the man said with a smile. "You could have even made a few coins—even coins made of *argentum* (_____silver_____). And I might have even given you a little *dōnum* (_____gift_____). Now there is a bigger mess that we have to clean up." At the word "mess," the man looked down at the two children.

The *vir* (_____man_____) lowered the scroll and looked *trāns viam* (__across the _____way_____).

On the other side of the street was a brazier—a fire pit made of *ferrum* (_____iron_____) that was ablaze with fire.

"But first I need to take care of this."

The *vir* (_____man_____) with the scroll walked over to the brazier and threw the scroll into the fire.

Fun Fact!

Most schools were a single room, and classes had about a dozen students. Rich families had their own teachers or slaves who would help their children in class.

A. Translation

1. **ob** in front of
2. **post** after
3. **propter** on account of
4. **inter** between
5. **contrā** against
6. **Docendō, discimus.** By teaching, we learn.

7. **praeter** past
8. **ante** before
9. **ad** to, toward
10. **ultrā** beyond
11. **trāns** across

B. Chant Fill in the accusative-preposition flowchart (in order).

Preposition	Meaning
ad	to, toward
ante	before
apud	at, by, near
circā	around
contrā	against
extrā	outside
infrā	below
inter	between, among
intrā	within
iuxtā	near, next to

Preposition	Meaning
ob	in front of
per	through
post	after
praeter	past
prope	near
propter	on account of
secundum	along
super	over, above, beyond
suprā	over, above, on top of
trāns	across
ultrā	beyond

C. Grammar Name two noun jobs that an accusative-case noun can fill.

1. direct object

2. object of the preposition

Derivatives

A. Study

Study the English derivatives that come from the Latin words you have learned this week:

Latin	English
ob	observe, oblong, obsess, obstruction
per	perfect, per chance, perennial, perspective, perceive, pertain, perspire
post	postpone
praeter	preternatural
prope	propinquity
secundum	second, secondary
super	supersonic, supercharge, supercomputer, superhuman, superhighway, supermarket, superpower, supersede, superstition, superior, superfluous, supercilious, superman
suprā	supranational
trāns	transport, transportation, transfer, transform, transact, translate, transmit, transitive
ultrā	ultraviolet, ultrared, ultraconservative, ultraliberal, ultralight

All of the words in this week's vocabulary list are prepositions. As you can see, there are many words in English that come from Latin prepositions. The Romans themselves created many compound words by combining a preposition with another word. Let's look at a few:

Preposition		Verb		New Verb	English
ob (against)	+	**struō** (I build)	=	**obstruō**	obstruct
per (through)	+	**spectō** (I look at)	=	**perspectō**	perspective
post (after)	+	**pōnō** (I put, place)	=	**postpōnō**	postpone
super (over)	+	**fluō** (I flow)	=	**superfluō**	superfluous
trāns (across)	+	**portō** (I carry)	=	**transportō**	transport

B. Apply

Now you're going to have an opportunity to see just how many English words come from Latin prepositions. In your dictionary, go to the *per*, *super*, and *trans* sections and find at least ten new words that are not in the list above. **Answers will vary. Potential answers (of which there could be many) are supplied.**

1. pertinent

2. supersensitive

3. pertinence

4. superior

5. perspicuous

6. superlative

7. perpetual

8. transient

9. persevere

10. transcontinental

A. New Vocabulary

Latin	English
ob	in front of
per	through
post	after
praeter	past
prope	near
propter	on account of
secundum	along
super	over, above, beyond
suprā	over, above, on top of
trāns	across
ultrā	beyond

B. Review Vocabulary

Latin	English
contrā	against
extrā	outside of
iuxtā	near, next to
inter	between
intrā	within

Chapter 25

Quiz

C. Chant   Fill in the accusative-preposition flowchart (in order).

Preposition	Meaning
ad	to, toward
ante	before
apud	at, by, near
circā	around
contrā	against
extrā	outside
infrā	below
inter	between, among
intrā	within
iuxtā	near, next to

Preposition	Meaning
ob	in front of
per	through
post	after
praeter	past
prope	near
propter	on account of
secundum	along
super	over, above, beyond
suprā	over, above, on top of
trāns	across
ultrā	beyond

D. Grammar   Name two noun jobs that an accusative-case noun can fill.

1. direct object

2. object of the preposition

Chapter 26

Another two weeks of study, and you have learned twenty-one new words—all of them prepositions! As you did during the last review week, make sure you have these words mastered. Check the boxes of each word you don't know. Then review those words as much as you need to in order to master them. For extra practice, write out the English translation next to each Latin word. Remember to look at the words while chanting them.

Chapter 24

❑ ad <u>to, toward</u>

❑ ante <u>before</u>

❑ apud <u>at, by, with</u>

❑ circā <u>around</u>

❑ contrā <u>against</u>

❑ extrā <u>outside of</u>

❑ infrā <u>below</u>

❑ inter <u>between</u>

❑ intrā <u>within</u>

❑ iuxtā <u>near, next to</u>

Chapter 25

❑ ob <u>in front of</u>

❑ per <u>through</u>

❑ post <u>after</u>

❑ praeter <u>past</u>

❑ prope <u>near</u>

❑ propter <u>on account of</u>

❑ secundum <u>along</u>

❑ super <u>over, above, beyond</u>

❑ suprā <u>over, above, on top of</u>

❑ trāns <u>across</u>

❑ ultrā <u>beyond</u>

Do you remember the chant for *sum, es, est*? Do you remember the chant for *eram, erās, erat*? How about *erō, eris, erit*? Study and chant the boxes below and make sure you have them mastered!

Present

	Singular	Plural
1st	**sum**: I am	**sumus**: we are
2nd	**es**: you are	**estis**: you all are
3rd	**est**: he/she/it is	**sunt**: they are

Imperfect

	Singular	Plural
1st	**eram**: I was	**erāmus**: we were
2nd	**erās**: you were	**erātis**: you all were
3rd	**erat**: he/she/it was	**erant**: they were

Future

	Singular	Plural
1st	**erō**: I will be	**erimus**: we will be
2nd	**eris**: you will be	**eritis**: you all will be
3rd	**erit**: he/she/it will be	**erunt**: they will be

Grammar Review   Past, present, and future of *sum*

Now you have learned the past (or imperfect), present, and future forms of *sum*. Study the boxes to the left, then make sure you can understand the sentences that are in the boxes to the right.

Imperfect

	Singular	Plural
1st	**eram**: I was	**erāmus**: we were
2nd	**erās**: you were	**erātis**: you all were
3rd	**erat**: he/she/it was	**erant**: they were

Eram amīcus. *I was a friend.*
Erās discipulus. *You were a student.*
Mārcus puer erat. *Marcus was a boy.*
Puerī erāmus. *We were boys.*
Virī puerī erant. *The men were boys.*

Present

	Singular	Plural
1st	**sum**: I am	**sumus**: we are
2nd	**es**: you are	**estis**: you all are
3rd	**est**: he/she/it is	**sunt**: they are

Sum magister. *I am a teacher.*
Discipula es. *You are a student.*
Amellia puella est. *Amellia is a girl.*
Germānī sumus. *We are brothers.*
Puellae amīcae sunt. *The girls are friends.*

Future

	Singular	Plural
1st	**erō**: I will be	**erimus**: we will be
2nd	**eris**: you will be	**eritis**: you all will be
3rd	**erit**: he/she/it will be	**erunt**: they will be

Erō magistra. *I will be a teacher.*
Amīcus eris. *You will be a friend.*
Iūlia magistra erit. *Julia will be a teacher.*
Discipulī eritis. *You all will be students.*
Puerī magistrī erunt. *The boys will be teachers.*

Translate the sentences below.

Sum agricola.
I am a farmer.

Sumus agricolae.
We are farmers.

Mārcus agricola et incola est.*
Marcus is a farmer and settler.

Nauta es.
You are a sailor.

Poēta erō.
I will be a poet.

Puer vir erit.
The boy will be a man.

Magistra bona erat.
The teacher was good.

Iūlia magistra mala erat.
Julia was a bad teacher.

Erāmus puerī.
We were boys.

Estis puellae.
You are girls.

Magistrī discipulī erant.
The teachers were students.

Puellae parvae discipulae erunt.
The small girls will be students.

*The word *et* means "and" in Latin.

Review

Object of the Preposition with the Accusative Case

The prepositions you have learned are usually followed by another word (a noun), which we call the object of the preposition. We label a preposition with *PR* and the object of the preposition with *OP*. Study the sentences below:

	SN	V	PR	OP		SN	V	PR	OP
	Mark walks to the school.					**Mārcus ambulat ad lūdum.**			

Do you see how the object of the preposition (OP) follows the preposition (PR) in both English and Latin? Do you see that *lūdum* is in the accusative case? All the prepositions that you learned recently go with the accusative case. We have already learned that the accusative case is used with direct objects (DO), as in the sentence *Mārcus amat lūdum* ("Marcus loves school"). Now we see that the accusative case can also be used as an object of the preposition!

Sentence Building: Study the sentences in the box and then translate the sentences below. Each sentence has a preposition that you have learned, and each is followed by a noun in the accusative case. After translating, label each sentence with SN, V, PR, and OP.

Magister ambulat ad discipulum. *The teacher walks to the student.*	**Servus extrā lūdum errat.** *The servant wanders outside of school.*	**Lūdus iuxtā forum est.** *The school is next to the forum.*
Fīlius ambulat ob lūdum. *The son walks in front of the school.*	**Germānus contrā germānum pugnat.** *Brother fights against brother.*	**Puellae per forum ambulant.** *The girls walk through the forum.*
Dominus circā forum ambulat. *The master walks around the forum.*	**Discipula ambulat inter amīcās.** *The student walks between (or among) friends.*	**Mārcus prope lūdum habitat.** *Marcus lives near the school.*

```
  SN    V    PR   OP
Mārcus ambulat ad magistrum.
```
Marcus walks to the teacher.

```
 SN    V    PR  OP
Pater ambulat ob casam.
```
Father walks in front of the house.

```
 SN   PR   OP    V
Puerī circā lūdum ambulant.
```
The boys walk around the school.

```
 SN   PR   OP   V
Equus extrā forum errat.
```
The horse wanders out of the forum.

```
SN  PR   OP   V
Vir contrā virum pugnat.
```
The man fights against the man.

```
 SN   PR   OP   V
Puella inter amīcās stat.
```
The girl stands among friends.

```
  SN      PR   OP  LV
Aedificium iuxtā agrum est.
```
The building is next to the field.

```
 SN  PR   OP   V
Puer per agrum errat.
```
The boy wanders through the field.

```
  SN    PR    OP    V
Puellae prope campum habitant.
```
The girls live near the plain.

Along the Appian Way, Part 21

As the scroll sat among the flames, Marcus couldn't believe what he was seeing. He still didn't know what was on the scroll, but he knew it had to be important.

He wrestled to get free, but the *bracchia* (_____arm_____) that held him squeezed tighter, pushing out his breath. As he gasped for air, he instinctively bit down on the *dūri* (_____hard_____), thick fingers pressed over his mouth.

The *vir* (_____man_____) holding him let go with a howl. Marcus sprinted forward.

The thug holding Julia reached out to grab Marcus, but Julia twisted and kicked the *vir* (_____man_____) hard in the ankle. He stumbled back as she wrenched free.

Marcus was *trāns viam* (_____across the road_____) in the blink of an eye. The tattooed *vir* (_____man_____) looked back and saw Julia running toward him as Marcus slipped behind his back. Using his foot, Marcus kicked the burning brazier, knocking it over.

The *vir* (_____man_____) jumped back as burning ash spilled out near his feet, singeing his toes.

The scroll rolled out onto the *humus* (_____ground_____), its edges burning. Marcus grabbed the scroll and beat out the flames.

"Come on!" Julia *clamābat* (_____shouted_____) and yanked Marcus away.

Grammar Lesson

The Second Irregular Verb: *eō, īre*

OK, it's time to learn another irregular verb. You remember what an **irregular verb** is, right? **It's a verb that doesn't follow the normal conjugation patterns for verbs.** Most irregular verbs are irregular because of changes in their stems. This week's irregular verb is a good example of this. *Eō, īre*, like *sum, esse*, is one of the most common verbs in the Latin language. It means "to go." Think about how often you say the verb "go" or "went" in your own conversation, and that will help you get a sense of how important this verb is. The most important thing to memorize with this verb is the present-tense endings. Notice that there are only two places where it's really different; can you find them?

Worksheet

A. Translation

1. **dōnō** _I give_

2. **pessimus** _worst_

3. **existimāmus** _we judge_

4. **nārrātis** _you all tell_

5. **ancillae** _maidservants_

6. **Dum spīrō, spērō.** _While I breathe, I hope._

7. **eō** _I go_

8. **glōria** _glory_

9. **rogābās** _you were asking_

10. **dūrus** _hard_

11. **optābit** _he/she will choose_

B. Chant
Give the present-tense verb forms for _eō, īre_ and fill in the boxes.

	Singular	Plural
1st person	eō: I go	īmus: we go
2nd person	īs: you go	ītis: you all go
3rd person	it: he/she/it goes	eunt: they go

C. Grammar
Define the following term and then answer the question.

1. Irregular verb:

A verb that doesn't follow any of the regular conjugation patterns.

2. What is it that makes most irregular verbs irregular?

changes in their stems

D. Derivatives

1. A ___pessimist___ always expects things to turn out for the worst. (_pessimus_)

2. If you don't want to participate, you have permission to ___opt___ out of the program. (_optō_)

A. New Vocabulary

Latin	English
rogō, rogāre, rogāvī, rogātum	I ask, to ask, I asked, asked
optō, optāre, optāvī, optātum	I choose, to choose, I chose, chosen
existimō, existimāre, existimāvī, existimātum	I judge, to judge, I judged, judged
dōnō, dōnāre, dōnāvī, dōnātum	I give, to give, I gave, given
eō, īre, īvī/iī, itum	I go, to go, I went, gone
altus, -a, -um	high
dūrus, -a, -um	hard
minimus, -a, -um	smallest
nūdus, -a, -um	bare
pessimus, -a, -um	worst

B. Review Vocabulary

Latin	English
dō, dare, dedī, datum	I give, to give, I gave, given
intrō, intrāre, intrāvī, intrātum	I enter, to enter, I entered, entered
labōrō, labōrāre, labōrāvī, labōrātum	I work, to work, I worked, worked
errō, errāre, errāvī, errātum	I wander, to wander, I wandered, wandered
stō, stāre, stetī, statum	I stand, to stand, I stood, stood

Quiz

C. Chant   Give the present-tense verb forms for *eō, īre* and fill in the boxes.

	Singular	Plural
1st person	eō: I go	īmus: we go
2nd person	īs: you go	ītis: you all go
3rd person	it: he goes	eunt: they go

D. Grammar   Give the definition or answer the question for each item below.

1. Irregular verb:

   A verb that doesn't follow any of the regular conjugation patterns.

2. What is it that makes most irregular verbs irregular?

   changes in their stems

The Romance Languages (cont.)

Here is a list of vocabulary words that shows how one Latin word leads to very similar words in many of the Romance languages.

English	Latin	Spanish	Portuguese	French	Italian	Romanian
arm	**bracchium**	brazo	braco	bras	braccio	brat
bed	**lectus**	lecho	leito	lit	letto	pat
book	**liber**	libro	livro	livre	libro	live
cow	**vacca**	vaca	vaca	vache	vacca	vaca
dead	**mortuus**	muerto	morto	mort	morto	mort
family	**familia**	familia	familia	famille	famiglia	familie
house	**domus/casa**	casa	casa	maison	casa	casa
language	**lingua**	lengua	lingua	langue	lingua	limba
moon	**lūna**	luna	lua	lune	luna	luna

Source: *Encyclopedia Britannica*, s.v. "Romance Languages."

Along the Appian Way, Part 22

Marcus and Julia only made it a few steps before the *īrātī virī* (___angry men___) grabbed their tunics, stopping them in their tracks. They struggled to get away, but the men yanked them off their feet.

In a flash of inspiration, Julia *clāmābat* (___shouted___) at the top of her voice. "THIEF! THIEF!"

All the surrounding townsfolk stopped what they were doing and *spectābant* (___looked at___) her.

The Roman soldiers who had passed by suddenly stopped and turned around.

All eyes were on Marcus, Julia, and the *malī virī* (___bad men___) that held them. The tattooed *vir* (___man___) looked nervous. He didn't know if they should hold the children or let them go.

Four of the Roman troops approached, led by a *vir* (___man___) in a purple robe. "Here, here. What claim of thievery is this? *Sum* (___I am___) Senator Marius. Tell me, what wrong has been done here?"

The *virī* (___men___) dropped the children and *stābant* (___stood___) there stiffly.

Marcus was first to speak. "These *virī* (___men___) stole this scroll from us. They tried to destroy something that was not theirs. What I say is *vērus* (___true___)."

Senator Marius looked at the *virī* (___men___) for their response. Just as their leader opened his mouth to respond, another voice was heard, "I've been looking all over for that!" Another man stepped from behind the senator. It was the messenger.

Grammar Lesson

Compound Verbs Formed with Prepositions

Eō, īre is very frequently combined with other words to form new words. When two smaller words come together to form one larger word, we call that a **compound word**. Compound verbs made by combining prepositions with common verbs are one of the most frequently encountered types of compound words. In fact, since last week's list included all of the accusa-

Worksheet

A. Translation

1. **plēnus** _full_

2. **mēnsa** _table_

3. **mēta** _turning point, goal_

4. **proximus** _nearest_

5. **serva** _female slave_

6. **Dum spīrō, spērō.** _While I breathe, I hope._

7. **amīca** _female friend_

8. **pūrus** _pure_

9. **rēctus** _straight_

10. **ultimus** _farthest_

B. Chant   Give the forms of _eō, īre._

	Present		Imperfect		Future	
	Singular	**Plural**	**Singular**	**Plural**	**Singular**	**Plural**
1st person	eō	īmus	ībam	ībāmus	ībō	ībimus
2nd person	īs	ītis	ībās	ībātis	ībis	ībitis
3rd person	it	eunt	ībat	ībant	ībit	ībunt

C. Grammar   Give the definition for each term or the English meaning for each Latin word below.

1. Compound word: _A word that is created by combining two smaller words._

2. **Trānsit:** _He goes across._

3. **Init:** _He enters._

4. **Subit:** _He goes under._

D. Derivatives

1. Trains and buses are forms of "mass ___transit___." (_trāns + eō, īre_)

2. At a feast, there is ___plenty___ of food to eat. (_plēnus_)

Derivatives

A. Study

Study the English derivatives that come from the Latin words you have learned this week:

Latin	English
plēnus	plenty, plenary, plenipotentiary
pūrus	pure, purify, purity, impure, impurity
rēctus	right, rectify, rectangle, rectitude, erect, correct, direct, director, rectum, rector, rectory
reliquus	relinquish, relic, reliquary, derelict, dereliction
proximus	proximate, approximate, approximately, proxy, proximity
ultimus	ultimate, ultimately, ultimatum
varius	various, variety, variable, invariable, vary, variegate

Fun Fact!

The names of our months come from the Romans. January, March, and June are named after gods, while July and August are named after famous Roman rulers. September through December are named after the number given to them in the original ten-month calendar.

B. Define

In a dictionary, look up two of the English derivatives from the list above and write their definitions in the spaces below:

1. _____

2. _____

C. Apply

From the seven Latin words in this week's vocabulary list come over thirty-five English words! Look at some of the words that come from *rēctus*—they are "straight" words. To *rectify* means to make straight or "set things straight" (make them right). A *rectangle* has four straight (and parallel) lines. Also, a *rectangle* has *right* angles. (The word "right" is also derived from *rēctus*.) *Rectitude* is rightness ("straightness") of principle or conduct. To *erect* something means to raise it up in a straight manner. To *correct* something (or someone) means to make it *right*. To *direct* means to arrange things in the *right* way. The *rectum* is the straight part of your large intestines.

1. What does a *director* do?

A director is someone who directs, controls, or supervises.

2. Look up the word "right" in your dictionary. How many different definitions are listed?

A good dictionary will have more than ten definitions.

A. New Vocabulary

Latin	English
plēnus, -a, -um	full
pūrus, -a, -um	pure
rēctus, -a, -um	straight
reliquus, -a, -um	remaining
proximus, -a, -um	nearest
ultimus, -a, -um	farthest
varius, -a, -um	various

B. Review Vocabulary

Latin	English
via, -ae	road, way
fossa, -ae	ditch
discipula, -ae	female student
domina, -ae	female master/mistress
famula, -ae	female servant

C. Chant   Give the tense endings of *eō, īre* and fill in the labels.

	Present		Imperfect		Future	
	Singular	Plural	Singular	Plural	Singular	Plural
1st person	eō	īmus	ībam	ībāmus	ībō	ībimus
2nd person	īs	ītis	ībās	ībātis	ībis	ībitis
3rd person	it	eunt	ībat	ībant	ībit	ībunt

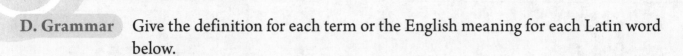

Quiz

D. Grammar Give the definition for each term or the English meaning for each Latin word below.

1. Compound word:

A word that is created by combining two smaller words.

2. **Trānsit:**

He goes across.

3. **Init:**

He goes in.

4. **Perit:**

He goes through.

Along the Appian Way, Part 23

The three men were restrained and put in manacles made of *ferrum* (____iron____). As they were led away, the messenger and the senator listened to the last of Marcus's and Julia's *fābula* (____story____). A big smile was on the messenger's face as he pulled a rather normal-looking scroll *ab* (____from____) his bag.

"I want to thank you, Marcus and Julia, for protecting this government scroll," said the messenger. "For on that scroll is an *epistula* (____letter____) proposing peace *cum* (____with____) one of our neighbors. This peace could stop many ongoing conflicts and save many lives. As an emissary of the Caesar himself, I thank you both."

"*Gaudeō* (____I rejoice____)!" said Julia, and quickly thrust out her hand for a handshake. Marcus chuckled silently, and the senator gave a polite nod. The messenger, however, grasped her hand firmly and solemnly shook it. He then shook Marcus's hand as well. Though Marcus didn't show it as much, he too *gaudēbat* (____rejoiced____).

"You should be granted a *praemium* (____reward____), for this *magnus* (____great____) and *dignus* (____worthy____) service," said the senator. He began to motion to one of his *virī* (____men____).

"No, no," Marcus said. "Our *praemium* (____reward____) is in doing the right thing." He bowed stiffly, then turned and *ambulābat* (____walked____) slowly away, clutching the lost scroll tightly.

Grammar Lesson

The Ablative Case

The ablative case has many uses, but perhaps the most important one is the one from which it gets its name: **Ab**-lative. Did you notice that it starts with the preposition *ab*, which means "from"? As a result, the ablative case is often used to express movement away from or separation from something else. Because of this, it frequently is used as the opposite of the accusative case, which is often used to express movement toward something. Sometimes the

A. Translation

1. **cōram** face-to-face with
2. **cum** with
3. **dē** down from, concerning, about
4. **ex** out of
5. **in + abl.** in, on
6. **Fāma volat.** Rumor flies.
7. **infrā** below
8. **prope** near
9. **super** over, above, beyond
10. **extrā** outside of
11. **prō** before, on behalf of

B. Chant Fill in the ablative-case preposition flowchart.

ā or ab	prae
cōram	prō
cum	sine
dē	sub
ē or ex	tenus
in	

C. Grammar For each preposition listed below, indicate whether it takes the accusative case, ablative case, or both.

1. **ab** ablative
2. **dē** ablative
3. **ad** accusative
4. **in** both
5. **trāns** accusative
6. **sub** both

D. Derivatives

1. If you want to leave, the _____ exit _____ is on the right. (*ex + eō, īre*)

2. A ship that can travel underwater is called a _____ submarine _____. (*sub*)

A. New Vocabulary

Latin	English
ā *or* ab	from, by, away from
cōram	face-to-face with
cum	with
dē	down from, concerning, about
ē *or* ex	out of
in + abl.	in
in + acc.	into
prae	in front of, before
prō	before, on behalf of
sine	without
sub + abl.	under
sub + acc.	up to
tenus	to the extent of, up to, down to, as far as

B. Review Vocabulary

Latin	English
apud	at, by, near
circā	around
contrā	against
extrā	outside of
infrā	below

C. Chant   Fill in the ablative-case preposition flowchart.

ā or ab	prae
cōram	prō
cum	sine
dē	sub
ē or ex	tenus
in	

D. Grammar   For each preposition listed below, indicate whether it is accusative case, ablative case, or both.

1. **prō** ___ablative___

2. **dē** ___ablative___

3. **prae** ___ablative___

4. **in** ___both___

5. **ultrā** ___accusative___

6. **sub** ___both___

Along the Appian Way, Part 24

"This belongs to you, *magister* (_____Master_____) Balbus," Marcus said as he *adībat* (____approached____) and presented the borrowed scroll *ad* (_____to_____) the professor. The professor didn't want to be pleased, but the thin smile that slipped onto his face gave away his pleasure as he took it back.

"I heard that you went on quite the adventure to get this back. Thank you for your diligence. You have proven yourself to be quite responsible and resourceful. I hope to see such *bonus* (_____good_____) work in class a bit more."

"Yes, sir."

Julia strolled along the smooth-cut *saxa* (_____rock_____) that made up the Appian *Via* (_____Way_____). With the midday sun shining on them, they both were quite *laetī* (_____happy_____).

Marcus looked at the coins of *argentum* (_____silver_____) that he now had in his hand. Since he no longer needed to pay for the scroll, the money he had earned was now his to spend however he wished.

"So, are we rich yet?" Julia asked as she skipped a pebble along the Roman *via* (_____road_____).

"I think we may be," Marcus replied, giving his coins a little jingle. "Yes, I most certainly think *sumus* (_____we are_____)!"

Marcus was thinking about what to do with his *argentum* (_____silver_____), but Julia *cogitābat* (____was thinking____) about riding an *equus* (_____horse_____) along the seashore. For a good while, the two of them *ambulabant in silentiō* (_____walked in silence_____) along the Appian *Via* (_____Way_____).

Grammar Lesson

Compound Verbs

Have you noticed that this week's list is all verbs? Normally we don't do this since we have you learn four Latin forms (called principal parts) for each verb, but we still thought this week's list would be a snap for you! That's

A. Translation Make sure to use the proper pronoun to go with each verb, and watch the tense of the forms of *sum*.

1. **eris** you will be

2. **accūsat** he/she accuses

3. **cēnāmus** we dine

4. **appellābam** I was naming

5. **erunt** they will be

6. **Fāma volat.** Rumor flies.

7. **commemorant** they remember

8. **cantābimus** we will sing

9. **erāmus** we were

10. **esse** to be

11. **sum** I am

B. Chant Fill in the tense endings of *sum* in the chart below.

	Present		Imperfect		Future	
	Singular	**Plural**	**Singular**	**Plural**	**Singular**	**Plural**
1st person	sum	sumus	eram	erāmus	erō	erimus
2nd person	es	estis	erās	erātis	eris	eritis
3rd person	est	sunt	erat	erant	erit	erunt

C. Grammar

1. The four _____principal_____ _____parts_____ are the forms of a word that are normally listed in a Latin dictionary.

2. Why is knowing the principal parts helpful? ___They help you use and translate the word.___

3. List the principal parts of the following words:

   a. **sum,** _____esse_____, _____fuī_____, _____futūrum_____

   b. **dō,** _____dare_____, _____dedī_____, _____datum_____

D. Derivatives

1. Johnny was _____absent_____ from school yesterday due to illness. (*absum*)

2. Don't _____accuse_____ someone of such a serious offense without evidence! (*accūsō*)

A. New Vocabulary

Latin	English
absum, abesse, āfuī, āfutūrum	I am absent, to be absent, I was absent, about to be absent
adsum, adesse, adfuī, adfutūrum	I am present, to be present, I was present, about to be present
abeō, abīre, abiī, abitum	I go away, to go away, I went away, gone
adeō, adīre, adiī, aditum	I approach, to approach, I approached, approached
exeō, exīre, exiī, exitum	I go out, to go out, I went out, gone out
cēnō, cēnāre, cēnāvī, cēnātum	I dine, to dine, I dined, dined
cantō, cantāre, cantāvī, cantātum	I sing, to sing, I sang, sung
appellō, appellāre, appellāvī, appellātum	I name, to name, I named, named
accūsō, accūsāre, accūsāvī, accūsātum	I accuse, to accuse, I accused, accused
commemorō, commemorāre, commemorāvī, commemorātum	I remember, to remember, I remembered, remembered

B. Review Vocabulary

Latin	English
erō	I will be
eram	I was
erunt	they will be

Quiz

C. Chant   In the chart below, fill in the tense endings of *sum*.

	Present		Imperfect		Future	
	Singular	**Plural**	**Singular**	**Plural**	**Singular**	**Plural**
1st person	sum	sumus	eram	erāmus	erō	erimus
2nd person	es	estis	erās	erātis	eris	eritis
3rd person	est	sunt	erat	errant	erit	erunt

D. Grammar   Answer the questions below.

1. The four ___principal___ ___parts___ are the forms of a word that are normally listed in a Latin dictionary.

2. Why is knowing the principal parts helpful? **They help you use and translate the word.**

3. Complete the list of the principal parts for each of the following.

     a. **eō,** īre, īvī, itum

     b. **absum,** abesse, āfuī, āfutūrum

Famous Palindrome: The *Sator* Square

Below is a famous Latin word square that has been found in many ancient sites throughout the former Roman Empire. It was found in the ancient city of Herculaneum, which was buried in AD 79 by ash from a volcano. It is also a palindrome because it can be read both forward and backward. In this case, the words can also be read top to bottom and bottom to top! See if you can read it all four ways!

Here are translations of the Latin words:

   sator: sower (as in "sower of seeds")
   Arepō: proper name of the sower (perhaps invented for the palindrome)
   tenet: holds
   opera: works or efforts
   rotās: wheels

S	A	T	O	R
A	R	E	P	O
T	E	N	E	T
O	P	E	R	A
R	O	T	A	S

The sentence reads: *Sator Arepō tenet operā rotās*, which can be translated as: "The sower Arepo holds with effort the wheels."

Here are a couple of palindromes in English: • Madam, I'm Adam • Race car

Can you invent your own palindrome? _____

Chapter 31

After another four weeks of study you have learned another forty words. As you did during the last review week, make sure you have these words mastered. Check the boxes of each word you don't know. Then review those words as much as you need to in order to master them. Remember to look at the words while chanting them.

Chapter 27	Chapter 29
❏ rogō __I ask__	❏ ā *or* ab __from, by, away from__
❏ optō __I choose__	❏ cōram __face-to-face with__
❏ existimō __I judge__	❏ cum __with__
❏ dōnō __I give__	❏ dē __down from, concerning, about__
❏ eō __I go__	❏ ē *or* ex __out of__
❏ altus, -a, -um __high__	❏ in + ablative __in__
❏ dūrus, -a, -um __hard__	❏ in + accusative __into__
❏ minimus, -a, -um __small__	❏ prae __in front of, before__
❏ nūdus, -a, -um __bare__	❏ prō __before, on behalf of__
❏ pessimus, -a, -um __worst__	❏ sine __without__
	❏ sub + ablative __under__
	❏ sub + accusative __up to__
	❏ tenus __to the extent of, up to, down to, as far as__

Chapter 28	Chapter 30
❏ plēnus, -a, -um __full__	❏ absum __I am absent__
❏ pūrus, -a, -um __pure__	❏ adsum __I am present__
❏ rēctus, -a, -um __straight__	❏ abeō __I go away__
❏ reliquus, -a, -um __remaining__	❏ adeō __I approach__
❏ proximus, -a, -um __nearest__	❏ exeō __I go out__
❏ ultimus, -a, -um __farthest__	❏ cēnō __I dine__
❏ varius, -a, -um __various__	❏ cantō __I sing__
	❏ appellō __I name__
	❏ accūsō __I accuse__
	❏ commemorō __I remember__

Review

Grammar Review   Present-Tense Irregular Verb—*eō, īre* (Ch. 27 & 28)

During the last unit, you learned the irregular verb *eō, īre*. Do you have it mastered?

	Singular	Plural
1st person	**eō**: I go	**īmus**: we go
2nd person	**īs**: you go	**ītis**: you all go
3rd person	**it**: he goes	**eunt**: they go

Do you remember the forms for *eō, īre* in the imperfect and the future? Here they are.

	Imperfect		Future	
	Singular	Plural	Singular	Plural
1st person	**ībam** I was going	**ībāmus** we were going	**ībō** I will go	**ībimus** we will go
2nd person	**ībās** you were going	**ībātis** you were going	**ībis** you will go	**ībitis** you will go
3rd person	**ībat** he was going	**ībant** they were going	**ībit** he will go	**ībunt** they will go

Note that in the imperfect and future forms, we simply add the imperfect and future endings to the letter *i*!

Translation Exercise   Study the box, then translate the sentences below.

Mārcus ad forum it.
 Marcus goes to the forum.

Puellae ad casam eunt.
 The girls go to the house.

Ad lūdum ībāmus.
 We were going to the school.

Ad monumentum eō.
 I go to the monument.

Ad fluvium ībis.
 You will go to the river.

Ad campum ībimus.
 We will go to the field.

Magister trāns viam ībat.
 The teacher was going across the street.

Jūlia ad lūdum it.

Julia goes to the school.

Puerī ad campum eunt.

The boys go to the level field.

Famulus trāns fluvium ībat.

The servant was going across the river.

Ad aedificium ībāmus.

We were going to the building.

Ad agrum eō.

I go to the field.

Ad vāllum ībis.

You will go to the wall.

Ad forum ībimus.

We will go to the forum.

Working with Prepositions (Ch. 29)

Object of the Preposition with the Ablative Case

Do you remember what a preposition is? *A preposition is a little word that connects a noun or a pronoun to the rest of the sentence* (see ch. 22). You have already learned prepositions such as *ad* ("to" or "toward"), and you learned that it takes the accusative case: *Jūlia ad lūdum ambulat* ("Julia walks to the school"). Now you have learned some prepositions that take the ablative case.

Prepositions in the accusative case often indicate motion toward (*Julia walks to the school*). Prepositions in the ablative case often indicate movement or motion away. Look at the sentence below. Remember that we label a preposition with a *PR* and the object of the preposition with an *OP*.

SN V PR   OP   SN   V   PR OP
Mark walks out of the school.   **Mārcus ambulat ex lūdō.**

Do you see how the object of the preposition (OP) follows the preposition (P) in both English and Latin? Do you see that *lūdō* is in the ablative case?

Sentence Building: Study the box, then translate the sentences below. Each sentence has a preposition that you have learned, and each is followed by a noun in the ablative or accusative case. After translating, label each sentence with *SN*, *V*, *PR*, and *OP*.

Magister ambulat ab lūdō. *The teacher walks from the school.*	**Discipulus in forum ambulat.** *The student walks into the forum.*	**Discipula ambulat sine amīcīs.** *The student walks without friends.*
Fīlius ambulat prae silvā. *The son walks in front of the forest.*	**Servus ex lūdō errat.** *The servant wanders out of school.*	**Dominus cōram famulō est.** *The master is face-to-face with the servant.*
Dominus in forum ambulat. *The master walks into the forum.*	**Germānus cum germānō pugnat.** *Brother fights with brother.*	

SN   V   PR OP
Mārcus ambulat ab campō.

Marcus walks from the level field. _____

SN   V   PR OP
Pater ambulat prae casā.

The father walks in front of the house. _____

SN PR OP   V
Puerī in lūdum ambulant.

The boys walk into the school. _____

SN PR OP V
Equus in forō errat.

The horse wanders in the forum. _____

SN PR OP V
Fīlius ex templō errat.

The son wanders out of the temple. _____

SN PR OP V
Vir cum virō pugnat.

The man fights with the man. _____

SN PR OP V
Puella sine amīcīs stat.

The girl stands without friends. _____

SN   PR OP V
Fēmina cōram fīliā est.

The woman is face-to-face with the daughter. _____

Review

Grammar Review   Review of *sum, esse*/Compound Verbs (Ch. 30)

	Present		Imperfect		Future	
	Singular	**Plural**	**Singular**	**Plural**	**Singular**	**Plural**
1st person	**sum** I am	**sumus** we are	**eram** I was	**erāmus** we were	**erō** I will be	**erimus** we will be
2nd person	**es** you are	**estis** you all are	**erās** you were	**erātis** you all were	**eris** you will be	**eritis** you all will be
3rd person	**est** he is	**sunt** they are	**erat** he was	**erant** they were	**erit** he will be	**erunt** they will be

Do you remember your chants for the verb *sum, esse* ("I am, to be")? Review the boxes above that contain the present, imperfect, and future forms for *sum, esse*. Can you chant them correctly with your eyes closed? Make sure you have these chants mastered.

Compound Verbs

We can easily build new verbs by adding a preposition to *sum, esse* or to *eō, īre*.

Preposition		Verb		New Verb	English
ab	+	**sum**	=	**absum**	**I am away, absent**
ad	+	**sum**	=	**adsum**	**I am present**
ab	+	**eō**	=	**abeō**	**I go away**
ad	+	**eō**	=	**adeō**	**I approach**
ex	+	**eō**	=	**exeō**	**I go out**
trāns	+	**eō**	=	**trānseō**	**I go across**
in	+	**eō**	=	**ineō**	**I go in, enter**

Study the sentences in the box, then translate the sentences below.

Puella abest. *The girl is away.*	**Puellae absunt.** *The girls are away.*	**Puerī adeunt ad lūdum.** *The boys approach the school.*

Famula abest.

The servant is away.

Fēminae absunt.

The women are away.

Agricolae ad silvam adeunt.

The farmers approach the forest.

Chapter 32

Review of Nouns

Congratulations! You have finished thirty-one weeks of Latin study. Do you realize that you have learned about 240 Latin words? In this last review chapter, we will give you another chance to show that you have mastered the Latin you have studied for the last thirty-one weeks. We will start with a review of nouns.

This year you have studied two kinds of nouns: first-declension nouns and second-declension nouns. Do you remember which declension is used for feminine nouns? That's right, the first declension. What declension is used primarily for masculine but also for neuter nouns? Yes, the second declension. You should be able to easily complete the boxes below. To check your work, turn to the noun charts in the reference section of your book.

First Declension, Feminine

Case	Singular	Plural
Nominative	**mēnsa**: table	**mēnsae**: tables
Genitive	**mēnsae**: of the table	mēnsārum: of the tables
Dative	mēnsae: to, for the table	**mēnsīs**: to, for the tables
Accusative	mēnsam: the table	mēnsās: the tables
Ablative	**mēnsā**: by, with, from the table	mēnsīs: by, with, from the tables

Second Declension, Masculine

Case	Singular	Plural
Nominative	**lūdus**: school	**lūdī**: schools
Genitive	**lūdī**: of the school	**lūdōrum**: of the schools
Dative	lūdō: to, for the school	lūdīs: to, for the schools
Accusative	lūdum: school	lūdōs: schools
Ablative	**lūdō**: by, with, from the school	lūdīs: by, with, from the schools

Do you remember the **neuter rule**? Any noun that is neuter will have the same endings in both the nominative and the accusative cases. If we have *dōnum* in the nominative (singular), then we will have *dōnum* in the accusative (singular). If we have *dōna* in the nominative (plural), then we will have *dōna* in the accusative (plural)!

Do you remember that nouns have three qualities—gender, number, and case?

For example, *mēnsa* is feminine, singular, and nominative.

End-of-Book Review

Second Declension, Neuter

Case	Singular	Plural
Nominative	**dōnum**: gift	**dōna**: gifts
Genitive	**dōnī**: of the gift	**dōnōrum**: of the gifts
Dative	dōnō : to, for the gift	dōnīs : to, for the gifts
Accusative	dōnum : the gift	**dōna**: the gifts
Ablative	dōnō : by, with, from the gift	dōnīs : by, with, from the gifts

Vocabulary Check

Let's see how you do with this small test of vocabulary. You should be able to score at least 75 percent on this test. If not, keep reviewing your vocabulary. The numbers preceding each word tell you what chapter the word comes from.

	Latin	English		Latin	English
1	**amō, amāre, amāvī, amātum**	I love, to love, I loved, loved	4	**puella, puellae**	girl
1	**fābula, fābulae**	story	4	**fīlia, fīliae**	daughter
1	**porta, portae**	gate	4	**domina, dominae**	master (f)/mistress
2	**via, viae**	road, way	6	**puer, puerī**	boy
2	**pātria, pātriae**	fatherland, country	6	**germānus, germānī**	brother
2	**rēgīna, rēgīnae**	queen	6	**servus, servī**	slave
3	**stō, stāre, stetī, statum**	I stand, to stand, I stood, stood	6	**lūdus, lūdī**	school, game
3	**īra, īrae**	anger	7	**vigilō, vigilāre, vigilāvī, vigilātum**	I guard, to guard, I guarded, guarded
3	**glōria, glōriae**	glory	7	**lupus, lupī**	wolf

Latin	English	Latin	English
8 ambulō, ambulāre, ambulāvī, ambulātum	I walk, to walk, I walked, walked	15 cibus, cibī	food
8 necō, necāre, necāvī, necātum	I kill, to kill, I killed, killed	15 fluvius, fluviī	river
8 dōnum, dōnī	gift	16 arō, arāre, arāvī, arātum	I plow, to plow, I plowed, plowed
9 oppidum, oppidī	town	16 flō, flāre, flāvī, flātum	I blow, to blow, I blew, blown
9 astrum, astrī	star	16 argentum, argentī	silver
9 gaudium, gaudiī	joy	17 ferrum, ferrī	iron
11 creō, creāre, creāvī, creātum	I create, to create, I created, created	17 saxum, saxī	rock
11 parvus, parva, parvum	small	17 vāllum, vallī	wall, rampart
11 dubius, dubia, dubium	doubtful	19 caveō, cavēre, cāvī, cautum	I guard against, to guard against, I guarded against, guarded against
12 bonus, bona, bonum	good	19 deus, deī	god
12 malus, mala, malum	bad	19 humus, humī	ground
12 novus, nova, novum	new	20 casa, casae	house
14 videō, vidēre, vīdī, vīsum	I see, to see, I saw, saw	20 epistula, epistulae	letter
14 nauta, nautae	sailor	20 templum, templī	temple
14 poēta, poētae	poet	21 audeō, audēre, ausus sum	I dare, to dare, I dared, dared
15 campus, campī	level space, plain, field	21 longus, longa, longum	long

End-of-Book Review

Latin	English	Latin	English
21 clārus, clāra, clārum	clear, famous	**27** optō, optāre, optāvī, optātum	I choose, to choose, I chose, chosen
22 dēfessus, dēfessa, dēfessum	tired	**27** dūrus, dūra, dūrum	hard
22 iūstus, iūsta, iūstum	just, fair, right	**28** plēnus, plēna, plēnum	full
22 mīrus, mīra, mīrum	strange, wonderful	**28** ultimus, ultima, ultimum	farthest
24 ad	to, toward	**29** ā _or_ ab	from, by
24 circā	around	**29** cōram	face-to-face with
24 inter	between, among	**29** cum	with
25 super	over, above, beyond	**30** adsum, adesse, adfuī, adfutūrum	I am present, to be present, I was present, about to be present
25 trāns	across	**30** abeō, abīre, abiī, abitum	I go away, to go away, I went away, went away
25 ultrā	beyond	**30** cēnō, cēnāre, cēnāvī, cēnātum	I dine, to dine, I dined, dined
27 rogō, rogāre, rogāvī, rogātum	I ask, to ask, I asked, asked		

Noun Jobs

Do you remember the jobs that nouns do? Try to match the correct noun job with the correct definition by drawing a line between them. Check your work by reviewing the text that comes afterward.

Subject Noun (SN) A noun that usually comes right after a preposition.

Object of the Preposition (OP) A person, place, or thing that is doing the action of the sentence or that is being renamed or described.

Direct Object (DO) A noun that renames the subject or tells us what the subject is.

Predicate Nominative (PrN) A noun that receives the action of a verb.

End-of-Book Review

Verbs: Present, Imperfect, and Future

You have learned many important verbs from two different patterns or conjugations: the first and the second conjugations. I am sure you remember that verbs are words that show action. Do you remember that verbs have three qualities: **person**, **number**, and **tense**? Do you remember that **tense is time**? Let's review tense first. Since tense is time, a verb's tense tells us what time it takes place—either in the past (imperfect), present, or future. Have you mastered the endings for all three tenses? Complete the boxes below to show that you have mastered these endings, then check your work against the reference section of your book.

First-Conjugation Forms

Present

	Singular	Plural
1st	amō	amāmus
2nd	amās	amātis
3rd	amat	amant

Imperfect

	Singular	Plural
1st	amā**bam**	amā**bāmus**
2nd	amābās	amābātis
3rd	amābat	amā**bant**

Future

	Singular	Plural
1st	amā**bō**	amābimus
2nd	amā**bis**	amābitis
3rd	amābit	amābunt

Second-Conjugation Forms

Present

	Singular	Plural
1st	videō	vidēmus
2nd	vides	vidētis
3rd	videt	vident

Imperfect

	Singular	Plural
1st	vidēbam	vidēbāmus
2nd	vidēbās	vide**bātis**
3rd	vidēbat	vide**bant**

Future

	Singular	Plural
1st	vidēbō	vide**bimus**
2nd	vidēbis	vidēbitis
3rd	vidēbit	vidēbunt

Label and translate the following Latin sentences into English. Each box contains verbs in all three tenses (present, future, and imperfect).

SN/V-T DO
Amō pātriam.

I love the native land/country.

Adj DO SN/V-T
Parvum oppidum videō.

I see the small town.

SN DO Adj V-T
Mārcus pātriam magnam amābit.

Marcus will love the big/great country.

SN DO AdJ V-T
Puerī monumentum magnum vidēbunt.

The boys will see the large monument.

DO Adj SN/V-T
Pātriam parvam amābās.

You used to love the small country.

SN DO Adj V-T
Mārcus saxum magnum vidēbat.

Marcus was seeing the large rock.

DO SN/V-T
Amīcōs vocō.

I call the friends.

DO Adj SN/V-T
Folium magnum habeō.

I have a large leaf.

SN DO V-T
Mārcus servōs vocābit.

Marcus will call the servants.

DO Adj SN/V-T
Epistulam parvam habēbitis.

You all will have a small letter.

SN DO V-T
Iūlia amīcās vocābat.

Julia was calling the friends.

SN DO Adj V-T
Iūlia epistulam longam habēbat.

Julia used to have a long letter.

End-of-Book Review

Verbs   Present, imperfect, and future of *sum, esse*; function of linking verbs (LV)

Review the forms of *sum, esse* below, then label and translate the sentences in the boxes on this page and the next.

Present

	Singular	Plural
1st	**sum**: I am	**sumus**: we are
2nd	**es**: you are	**estis**: you all are
3rd	**est**: he is	**sunt**: they are

Imperfect

	Singular	Plural
1st	**eram**: I was	**erāmus**: we were
2nd	**erās**: you were	**erātis**: you all were
3rd	**erat**: he was	**erant**: they were

Future

	Singular	Plural
1st	**erō**: I will be	**erimus**: we will be
2nd	**eris**: you will be	**eritis**: you all will be
3rd	**erit**: he will be	**erunt**: they will be

PrN SN/LV
Puella es.

You are a girl.

SN LV PrN Adj
Jūlia est fēmina laeta.

Julia is a happy woman.

SN PrN LV
Iūlia magistra erit.

Julia will be a teacher.

SN PrN LV
Mārcus discipulus erat.

Marcus was a student.

SN LV PrA
Epistula est bona.

The letter is good.

SN LV PrA
Caelum erit clārum.

The sky will be clear.

SN/LV PrN
Sum discipulus.

I am a student.

SN/LV PrN
Estis agricolae.

You all are farmers.

SN/LV PrN
Sumus nautae.

We are sailors.

SN/LV PrN
Erimus inimīcī.

We will be enemies.

SN/LV PrN
Eritis amīcī.

You all will be friends.

SN LV PrA
Saxa sunt magna.

The rocks are large.

Parse, label, and translate the sentences on this page.

SN LV PrN
Iūlia est puella.
Nom/S/F 3/S/Pr Nom/S/F

Julia is a girl.

SN LV PrA
Iūlia est parva.
Nom/S/F 3/S/Pr Nom/S/F

Julia is small.

SN/LV PrN
Es germāna.
2/S/Pr Nom/S/F

You are a sister.

SN/LV PrA
Eris serēna.
2/S/F Nom/S/F

You will be calm.

SN PrN LV
Mārcus fīlius est.
Nom/S/M Nom/S/M 3/S/Pr

Marcus is a son.

SN PrA LV
Mārcus serēnus erat.
Nom/S/M Nom/S/M 3/S/I

Marcus was calm.

SN PrN LV
Mārcus germānus est.
Nom/S/M Nom/S/M 3/S/Pr

Marcus is a brother.

PrA SN/LV
Īrātus es.
Nom/S/M 2/S/Pr

You are angry.

PrN SN/LV
Discipulus erās.
Nom/S/M 2/S/I

You were a student.

SN SN PrA LV
Mārcus et Iūlia īrātī sunt.
Nom/S/M Nom/S/F Nom/P/M 3/P/Pr

Marcus and Julia are angry.

SN SN LV PrN
Mārcus et Iūlia sunt amīcī.*
Nom/S/M Nom/S/F 3/P/Pr Nom/P/M

Marcus and Julia are friends.

SN SN PrA LV
Mārcus et Iūlia dēfessī erant.
Nom/S/M Nom/S/F Nom/P/M 3/P/I

Marcus and Julia were tired.

*The word *et* means "and."

Prepositions

Do you remember what a preposition is? **It is a part of speech that connects a noun or pronoun to the rest of the sentence.** Prepositions are usually little words such as "to," "with," "from," "out," "in," "into," and so on. In Latin, they tend to be little words, too (*ad, cum, ab, ex, in,* and so on). Review your lists of prepositions in chapters 24, 25, and 29, then parse, label, and translate the sentences below.

Prepositions with the accusative case

SN PR OP V
Iūlia ad casam ambulat.
Nom/S/F Acc/S/F 3/S/Pr

Julia walks to the house.

SN PR OP V
Iūlia circā forum ambulat.
Nom/S/F Acc/S/N 3/S/Pr

Julia walks around the forum.

SN   SN PR OP   V
Mārcus et Dāvus extrā silvam ambulant.
Nom/S/M Nom/S/M   Acc/S/F 3/P/Pr

Marcus and David walk outside the forest.

PR   OP   SN/V
Post Dāvum ambulābātis.
Acc/S/M   2/P/I

You all were walking after David.

SN PR OP V
Mārcus iuxtā forum habitat.
Nom/S/M   Acc/S/N 3/S/Pr

Marcus lives near the forum.

PR OP SN/V
Trāns viam ambulābis.
Acc/S/F 2/S/F

You will walk across the road.

Prepositions with the ablative case

SN PR OP V
Iūlia cum Mariā ambulābat.
Nom/S/F Abl/S/F 3/S/I

Julia was walking with Maria.

SN PR OP V
Iūlia in silvā cantat.
Nom/S/F Abl/S/F 3/S/Pr

Julia sings in the forest.

PR OP   SN/V
Ē casā ambulābāmus.
Abl/S/F 1/P/I

We were walking out of the house.

SN PR OP V
Lupus in silvā ambulat.
Nom/S/M Abl/S/F 3/S/Pr

The wolf walks in the forest.

SN V PR OP
Equus est cōram lupō.
Nom/S/M 3/S/Pr Abl/S/M

The horse is face-to-face with the wolf.

SN PR OP V
Equus ē silvā ambulat.
Nom/S/M Abl/S/F 3/S/Pr

The horse walks out of the forest.

Adjectives

Do you remember what an adjective is? **It is that part of speech that describes or modifies other nouns** (see chapter 11). Adjectives answer one of three questions: What kind? Which one? and How many? Parse, label, and translate the following sentences.

SN LV PrN Adj
Iūlia est puella parva.
Nom/S/F 3/S/Pr Nom/S/F Nom/S/F

Julia is a small girl.

SN/LV PrN Adj
Estis discipulae bonae.
2/P/Pr Nom/P/F Nom/P/F

You all are good students.

SN PrN Adj LV
Mārcus fīlius magnus erit.
Nom/S/M Nom/S/M Nom/S/M 3/S/F

Marcus will be a big son.

SN PrN Adj LV
Mārcus fīlius bonus est.
Nom/S/M Nom/S/M Nom/S/M 3/S/Pr

Marcus is a good son.

SN SN PrN Adj LV
Mārcus et Iūlia amīcī bonī sunt.
Nom/S/M Nom/S/F Nom/P/M Nom/P/M 3/P/Pr

Marcus and Julia are good friends.

SN PR OP Adj V
Iūlia ad forum magnum ambulat.
Nom/S/F Acc/S/N Acc/S/N 3/S/Pr

Julia walks to the big forum.

DO Adj SN/V
Vāllum magnum creābimus.
Acc/S/N Acc/S/N 1/P/F

We will create a big wall.

SN DO Adj V-T
Mārcus monumentum dignum videt.
Nom/S/M Acc/S/N Acc/S/N 3/S/Pr

Marcus sees the worthy monument.

SN DO Adj V-T
Iūlia silvam dūram explōrābat.
Nom/S/F Acc/S/F Acc/S/F 3/S/I

Julia was exploring the harsh forest.

SN SN V DO Adj
Mārcus et Iūlia vītant silvam ignōtam.
Nom/S/M Nom/S/F 3/P/Pr Acc/S/F Acc/S/F

Marcus and Julia avoid the
unknown forest.

Continue the series!

If you complete all three Latin for Children primers you will:

- learn 720 commonly used Latin vocabulary words.
- master 75% of Latin grammar.
- read substantial stories in Latin.
- know more than 1,500 English words derived from Latin, and be able to deduce many more!
- be prepared to begin reading original Latin.
- gain a head start to learning Spanish, French, or other Romance languages.
- understand Latin on monuments, sculptures, dollar bills, and more.
- be prepared to take the National Latin Preparatory or Vocabulary exam.

Revised and continually sharpened since 2001, the award-winning Latin for Children curriculum continues to be a strong, inviting, and creative program designed to introduce upper-grammar-school students to Latin.

Your Latin Journey

Lower Grammar

You Can *Start* Here ↘

Grades 1–2

Grades 2–3

Upper Grammar

Start or Continue *Here* ↘

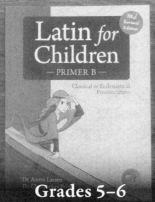

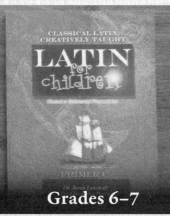

Grades 4–5

Grades 5–6

Grades 6–7

Ready for **National Latin Exam Prep**

Middle & High School

or Here ↘

Grades 7–8+

Grades 8–9+

Grades 9–10+

Grades 10–Adult

Ready for

| National Latin Exam Level I | National Latin Exam Level II | National Latin Exam Level III or IV Prose | National Latin Exam Level III or IV Prose |